JENSEN FAMILY BALLPARK QUEST

How We Visited All 30 MLB Ballparks

Yates Jensen

Copyright © 2024 by Yates R. Jensen Jr.
All rights reserved.
No portion of this book may be reproduced in any form without written permission from the publisher or author, except as permitted by U.S. copyright law.
This publication is designed to provide accurate and authoritative information in regard to the subject matter covered. It is sold with the understanding that neither the author nor the publisher is engaged in rendering legal, investment, accounting or other professional services. While the publisher and author have used their best efforts in preparing this book, they make no representations or warranties with respect to the accuracy or completeness of the contents of this book and specifically disclaim any implied warranties of merchantability or fitness for a particular purpose. No warranty may be created or extended by sales representatives or written sales materials. The advice and strategies contained herein may not be suitable for your situation. You should consult with a professional when appropriate. Neither the publisher nor the author shall be liable for any loss of profit or any other commercial damages, including but not limited to special, incidental, consequential, personal, or other damages.
Book Cover by Yates R. Jensen Jr.
Photographs by Yates R. Jensen Jr.
First edition 2024

JENSEN FAMILY BALLPARK QUEST

Preface:
Chapter 1 - 2014 - Can We Really Do This?
Chapter 2 - "Let's Get It Started"
Chapter 3 - Stadium #2 Philadelphia - Citizens Bank Park
Chapter 4 - The Big Apple, Stadium #3 (New) Yankee Stadium
Chapter 5 - Cooperstown and the Hall of Fame
Chapter 6 - Boston #4 Fenway Park! So Good, So Good, So Good!
Chapter 7 - Back to NYC #5 New York Mets' CitiField
Chapter 8 - Baltimore #6 Camden Yards
Chapter 9 - Finally, Home, Sweet Home! - Year One Complete
Chapter 10 - 2015 - #7 Great American Ballpark - Cincinnati
Chapter 11 - Stadium #8 Comerica Park - Detroit
Chapter 12 - Stadium #9 - Rogers Centre - Toronto
Chapter 13 - Niagara Falls!
Chapter 14 - Cleveland Rocks! - #10 Progressive Field
Chapter 15 - "The Steel City" - #11 - Pittsburgh's PNC Park
Chapter 16 - 2016 - #12 Loan Depot Park and #13 Tropicana Field
Chapter 17 - 2018 - FanFest - #14 Nationals Park
Chapter 18 - All-Star Workout Day and Home Run Derby Day!
Chapter 19 - FanFest and The All-Star Game!
Chapter 20 - Capital Tour and Braves at Nationals Game
Chapter 21 - 2019 - The Midwestern Tour - #15 Busch Stadium
Chapter 22 - #16 - Kauffman Stadium - Kansas City
Chapter #23 - "Is this Heaven?" - Field of Dreams
Chapter 24 - Minneapolis Minnesota - Stadium #17 Target Field
Chapter 25 - Wisconsin Wonders, Lambeau and #18 Miller Park
Chapter 26 - The Windy City - #19 Wrigley Field
Chapter 27 - Tour of Wrigley and #20 Guaranteed Rate Field
Chapter 28 - 2021 - COVID Break and #21 Coors Field - Colorado
Chapter 29 - Head for the Rockies!
Chapter 30 - Amarillo By (Evening) Sorry George Strait
Chapter 31 - A Couple Days in Amarillo
Chapter 32 - Arlington, Texas - #22 Globe Life Field - Texas Rangers
Chapter 33 - Stadium #23 - Houston Astros' Minute Maid Park
Chapter 34 - 2022 - The West Coast - The Grand Canyon
Chapter 35 - Phoenix and #24 Chase Field - Arizona Diamondbacks
Chapter 36 - San Diego and Stadium #25 - Petco Park

Chapter 37 - The Pacific Coast Highway and #26 - Angels Stadium
Chapter 38 - "I Love LA!" - Tour of the sites in Los Angeles
Chapter 39 - #27 - Dodger Stadium
Chapter 40 - San Francisco and #28 - Oracle Park
Chapter 41 - #29 - The Oakland Coliseum
Chapter 42 - 2024 - The Emerald City - #30 - Seattle's T-Mobile Park
Chapter 43: "The Walk Off"
<u>My Top 10 List</u>

DEDICATIONS:

This book is dedicated to the ones that helped make it all possible.

To Tammy, my loving wife, none of this would have been possible without your persistence, your planning, your coordination, your patience and open-mindedness, and your unwavering and unending love for our family.

To Trey and Tate, may this always be a reminder of the incredible journey that we undertook as a family and may it always bring back fond memories of all the experiences we had.

And to the thousands of fine folks that work at all the ballparks across America - the parking attendants, ticket takers, security guards, ushers, concession stand workers, vendors in the stands, game day administrators, and front office staff, thank you for continuing to provide the ballpark experience to everyone on a daily basis. It most definitely can not be done without you!

PREFACE:

"Baseball, it is said, is only a game. True. And the Grand Canyon is only a hole in Arizona." - Journalist & Author, George Will

My name is Yates Jensen and I am a baseball fan. And no, I am not trying to introduce myself like I am at an AA meeting, although some might say I do have an addiction. I am a retired high school history teacher who taught and coached multiple sports, including baseball, for over 28 years in the foothills of North Carolina. I retired in 2022 and had a very rewarding career that I look back on quite fondly. My wife, Tammy, and I have two sons - Trey and Tate. Our family really started to fall in love with the game of baseball around the time Trey turned 9 and Tate turned 7. And we are all Atlanta Braves fans, even though Tate's allegiance when he was younger bounced around to a few different teams. This is the story of how we came up with the idea of seeing every Major League ballpark before our sons graduated from high school.

I never considered myself a writer, but in 2014 my family embarked on a monumental quest of trying to watch a Major League Baseball game at all 30 ballparks across the United States. I knew this would be a challenging adventure that would take a family of four several years to complete. So, in 2014 when we started this, I had the wherewithal to write about our trips in a blog that I would update after every phase was completed each year. My main goal in doing the blog was so that my sons would have something to look back on when they are older to help them remember each ballpark as well as all the wonderful adventures we had. I included many pictures of ballparks as well as sites that we visited along the way. Fortunately, I was able to keep up with this task as we checked stadiums off the list each year. Little did I know there would be so much interest in my blog as I posted each entry on my FaceBook page and allowed others to share in our adventures. Then, "The Paper", which is the actual name of a weekly newspaper in our area, decided to run a story about our family completing the goal of seeing all 30 MLB Ballparks. And then I thought, maybe others would also be interested and would like to read about our story.

So, when we completed our quest in August of 2024, I had the idea of putting all of my blog entries into a book, again so my sons would have something to refer back to in the future and also so that anyone who was interested could read about our trips. Which is why you are reading this now I suppose. I did struggle over how to title this ebook. I decided to use the word quest because there were times when we doubted that we could pull this off. And it was such a long and involved series of journeys that the goal of 30 ballparks really did become an 11 year long quest.

This really was the adventure of a lifetime. We were able to see so much of this great country and meet so many wonderful people. I will cherish the memories we made forever. So, Thank You for taking an interest in our story. I hope you enjoy it.

-Yates Jensen Jr.

CHAPTER 1 - CAN WE REALLY DO THIS?

Have you ever had an idea that seemed almost impossible at the time, but turned into a major goal that bordered on obsession? That is what happened to me and my family beginning in the summer of 2014. I was a 44 year-old high school history teacher and basketball coach, living in the North Carolina Foothills,. I was married to my lovely wife, Tammy, of 10 years, and father of two young boys - Trey (age 9) and Tate (age 7). Our boys were just learning to appreciate America's greatest pastime - the great game of baseball. They had just started playing organized baseball and we were becoming a baseball family. Little did we know that it would become our passion, one that we hold on to still to this day. (Both boys would later continue to play travel ball, middle school baseball, high school baseball, showcase baseball, and eventually, college baseball) Our boys even built their own wiffle ball field in our backyard. Rarely did a day go by when they were not out there playing or we were not doing something baseball related. And we loved it!

So, in deciding what our 2014 summer plans would be, my wife and I knew that we would have to do something involving baseball. We thought, how about a trip to a baseball game? Of course, that sounds fun. After all, the boys are getting old enough to really enjoy going to a Major League game. We were all huge Atlanta Braves fans and we tried not to miss a game on TV. And we had already been to Turner Field in Atlanta on Memorial

Day to see the Braves and Red Sox. But, we had the rest of the summer with nothing planned.

So then my wife and I (really my wife - Tammy gets all the credit) thought about making a trip to Cooperstown, NY. But why Cooperstown in 2014? Well, as I said, we were huge fans of the Atlanta Braves. It was announced in January of 2014 that several of our former beloved Atlanta Braves (Greg Maddux, Tom Glavine, and Bobby Cox) were going to be inducted into the Baseball Hall of Fame, When I heard that, it kind of became a pipe dream of mine to go to Cooperstown in July to see the induction ceremony. But that would be a long way for us living in North Carolina, and is it really worth going that far just for the Hall of Fame? And I thought to myself, "for any true baseball fan, it was!" Then the practical side of me thinking about the logistics of getting a family of four with two young boys all the way to New York reared its head and I did not give it much thought after that. But my lovely and thoughtful wife who loves a challenge started thinking. "What if we make it a trip to see several games? I think the boys would love it". "Yes we will!!" I said.

And that is how this dream began. The quest was conceived. The challenge was made. We decided that our mission was going to be to take the boys to see a game at all 30 Major League Ballparks and to complete it before our oldest son, Trey, graduates from high school in 2023. A pretty lofty goal for our young family of four, but as you will see, we were up for the challenge. To do something like this was going to take a lot of planning. And we would have to do it in phases based on the geography and location of all 30 MLB Stadiums. The first area that we planned on covering was what I call the Northeast. All the stadiums around New York due to going to Cooperstown would be the goal for year one.

Now Tammy is not known to do things halfway. If she is going to do something, she is going to do it right with lots of pre-planning and forethought put in ahead of time. She found out when the induction ceremony would be in Cooperstown and got the MLB baseball schedule out and got right to work. She had maps and charts and spreadsheets and calendars and after a few days, she came up with a plan so thought out that it would make any military commander proud. What she came up with seemed impossible at the time. She suggested that we go to Philadelphia for a Phillies/SF Giants game, head up to NYC for a Yankees/Blue Jays game, and then over to Cooperstown for a couple of days for the Hall of Fame ceremonies. Leave there and go to Boston for a Red Sox/Blue Jays game, go back to New York for a Mets/Phillies game. Head down to Washington and Baltimore to see the Nats and Orioles. Wow! Just the idea of all of that seemed logistically impossible. Can we really do this? If there is anything that gets my wife motivated, it's the idea of a challenge. Well, here we go. We left our own friendly confines of our Rutherford College, NC home on Wednesday July 23rd, 2014. "Man, this is going to be awesome!", I thought, "but can we pull it off?

◆ ◆ ◆

Points of Clarification

As we set the goal for the boys to see all 30 Major League Teams in their home ballparks before Trey (9) graduates from high school, for numerical purposes, we are going to count Atlanta's Turner Field and later, Truist Park, as Ballpark #1 for the boys as they had been there and would go there several times throughout this journey. The Braves opened up a new park on March 29, 2018 called Truist Park, which, ironically, is where we also happened to be when we not only got to see the very first game in a brand new ballpark, (which was pretty cool) but also got to see Nick Markakis hit a game-winning walk off homerun to beat the Phillies in the Braves brand new ballpark! We would go on to become season ticket "A-List" members and, of course,, we would go to many games at Truist throughout this adventure. So, for the sake of the count, it, too, will also be considered Stadium #1.

Before the boys came along, I had been to a few other ballparks. When I was a kid, my parents had taken me to Atlanta's Fulton County Stadium a few times, and I had been to a game in Houston's Minute Maid park back before I got married. And before Tammy and I had kids, as a surprise gift, she took me to see one of the greatest rivalries in professional sports, a Yankees/Red Sox game at the old Yankee Stadium. In fact, we were at the game where Derek Jeter dove head first into the stands to make a play and ended up breaking his nose. On another trip when the boys were very small, we went to St. Louis to visit Tammy's sister and I went to a game at Busch Stadium to see the Cardinals with my brother-in-law, Chantz. But we are not going to count those stadiums in our quest as the goal had become to get the boys to see all 30 current Major League ballparks.

Throughout this journey, I will make mention several times of the Hickory Crawdads, which is a Single A Minor League team close to where we live (about 15 minutes away). We go to several games each year. Many former Crawdads have made it to the Major Leagues and we will see several of them play on this trip and I like to mention them in my story to show relevance for the boys.

Let me also remind you that I was a History teacher. And for me, this journey would be twofold. If we are going to visit all of these cities, there are going to be so many opportunities to take little mini-history "field trips" along the way. So be prepared for some stories about some historical places that we will visit throughout this journey. To borrow a line from Doctor Seuss, "oh, the places we will go"!

CHAPTER 2 - "LET'S GET IT STARTED"

Year 1, July 23, 2014 - The first day we left home at about 10:00 AM heading to Philadelphia. We knew it would be a long drive so we had the Minivan packed and stocked with plenty of snacks for all and movies to entertain the boys. We decide to head up I-77 into Virginia and then take I-81 up through the Shenandoah Valley. What a beautiful drive. Of course that area is rich in historical sites that I am just itching to see but my traveling companions would be bored out of their minds, besides we have to get to Philly and get a room in order to get to the game the next day. So I keep the hammer down.

Now here is where I need to interject a very important piece of information. As I mentioned in the previous post, my wife Tammy is a planner. She likes to have itineraries prepared well in advance before we ever leave town. But for this trip, she has only a baseball schedule and list of driving times from place to place in hand. This was a little disconcerting for me. "You mean we don't have reservations at hotels? No baseball game tickets pre-purchased?" I was comforted with the reply of "we'll be fine".

Well, I wasn't so sure about that. After all, we both had smartphones. We had all the information we needed right in the palm of our hands. It turns out those phones are extremely handy.

On the way up to Philadelphia I thought it would be neat to stop over in Hershey so the boys could see where some of their favorite candies were made. We got there and did the little "ride on" tour of the factory which disembarked right there in the candy store. And of course we had to get some Hershey's candy made right there in Hershey PA. Check! The boys thought it was awesome.

Next, it was on to Philly to find accommodations. We, or I, had decided to use Hotels.com to find a room. It was a very useful website that allowed us to pick a room based on what we were looking for. We had found a couple of options in the neighborhood called King of Prussia located just west of the city. Instead of booking online we decided to drive by the places first before committing. We looked at some mid range hotels like Best Western and Holiday Inn but on the way in we spotted a Motel 6. It looked pretty nice and seemed to be in a safe location. We only needed it for one night and then we would be on our way. Oh boy! Sorry Tom Bodett but you can leave the light OFF for us from now on. Kind of weird when a hotel room has laminate flooring throughout. Tammy was concerned about bed bugs. It was late and we were tired so we decided to stay and make the best of it. We survived the night with an important lesson learned. I don't mean to sound uppity or anything, but discount rate hotels are discounted for a reason.

Not a big deal because the next day we would begin an epic quest that will lead to many awesome experiences!

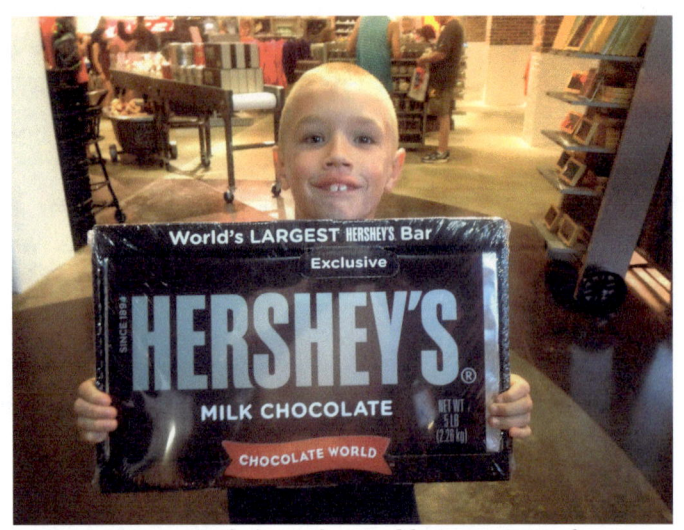

Trey pretty excited about the World's Largest Hershey Bar

CHAPTER 3 - STADIUM #2 PHILADELPHIA - CITIZENS BANK PARK

The City of Brotherly Love. After surviving the night at the Motel 6, we were ready to get going pretty early. We drove into the city and found the Philadelphia Sports Complex. I have to give credit to Philadelphia for their city planning. Every major sports team's home facilities are right there in the same area and there is adequate parking for each. Since we arrived so early the parking attendant said she was not charging yet so we didn't have to pay to park. Score! There was a subway station at the Sports Complex which was at the south side of the city. We decided to ride up into the city to see the sights. After all, the Social Studies teacher in me had to go show the boys the areas where our country was founded.

We exited the subway in the heart of the historic district. The Liberty Bell and Independence Hall were in plain sight. We saw the Bell and then took the tour of Independence Hall. What a moving experience for me. To be right there where the founding fathers were deciding on the course for our great nation. Wow! I was reminded of Nicholas Cage running through there in National Treasure, proof that I watch too many movies I guess.

Independence Hall where the Declaration was discussed and signed.

Then back on the subway to Citizens Bank Park, home of the Phillies. As a Braves fan, I wasn't too excited about seeing the Phils but it was our first ballpark on the big baseball trip so we were ready. We grabbed some lunch and of course, what do you eat while in Philadelphia - a Philly Cheesesteak! Tate and I were very impressed with the meal.

Citizens Bank is a very nice stadium full of the rich Phillies history and in some ways it reminded me of Turner Field. We got our tickets in the upper deck and got ready for the 1:05 game where Cole Hamels would be pitching against former Brave Tim Hudson of the Giants. It was great to see "Huddy" although it was hard to see him in that Giants uniform. The temperature was hot as you would expect for an afternoon game in July. The game was a pitchers' dual. Both starters were sharp. The Phillies won the game 2-1. We didn't see the end as we headed down with the boys to line up for the Kids Run the Bases activity at the conclusion of the game. We couldn't miss an opportunity for the boys to run around the bases at Citizens Bank.

Tate and Trey at Stadium #2 - Citizens Bank Ballpark in Philadelphia. This pose would become the standard at most parks, and one that the boys would dred but eventually learn to tolerate

Tate and Trey running the bases and seen on the "big screen"

Our time in Philly was enjoyable for the most part. We got to combine some history with some baseball and got the first stadium checked off. On to New Jersey to find a room for the next two nights. Again using our handy dandy Hotels.com app we were able to find a room in Secaucus at the Holiday Inn Express. It turned out to be a really nice place with easy access to NYC.

CHAPTER 4 - THE BIG APPLE, STADIUM #3 (NEW) YANKEE STADIUM

The next day it was time to take in the big city. Tammy and I were excited to show the boys NYC and they were excited to see it. Now I'm not going to lie, I am a little intimidated by large urban areas, not to mention the largest one in the US. So I was not going to drive. We were staying in Secaucus, NJ which enabled us to take a bus right into the city via the Lincoln Tunnel. We arrived at the Port Authority Bus Terminal which is at 42nd street and very close to Times Square. It was mid-morning and we had planned to be in the city all day and head up to the Bronx for the Yankees game that evening. So we start walking and walking. It was fun to see the sights and especially to see the faces of Trey and Tate. Tammy, being the responsible mom, had instructed the boys (and me) that they were to hold mom and dad's hand at all times (Tate, of course, would be the one who would need to be reminded of this rule several times). Trey was just fine with it. Tammy writes her cell number on the boys' arms should they get separated from us (she is a great Mom!).

"Can we see NYC in one day?" I thought. Well, not adequately, but we were going to give it our best shot. We set out into Times Square and take in all the sites. We see all the electronic billboards, the place where the ball dropped on New Years Eve, and of course, the Naked Cowboy, which Tate (and Tammy too I think) got a kick out of. We head to Rockefeller Plaza, St. Patrick's

Cathedral, Grand Central Station, and over to The Empire State Building. The boys wanted to see The Statue of Liberty which was at the southernmost part of Manhattan so that meant we needed to take the subway. Here was a part of New York culture I thought the boys needed to see. And here was where we looked the most like tourists because as you may know it can be confusing.

We make it to the correct station and get out to Battery Park to get a view of Lady Liberty. The boys finally feel like they have seen something they can identify New York City with. We go by the 9/11 Memorial and try to explain to them what it is about. We walk up through the financial district, see the big bull, and get back on the subway headed to the Bronx and Yankee Stadium.

The Statue of Liberty

Ah, the main reason for coming here. We arrived in the Bronx and made our way to the New Yankee Stadium. I have to say I had some mixed emotions as we approached the stadium. I still remember the Braves' World Series losses to the Yankees in the 90s and yes, it still stings.

Upon first glance, the ballpark was quite impressive. It was what I would call a "diamond in the rough". It is a beautiful facility located in a not-so-beautiful part of the city. We get our tickets and head in. The guy taking our tickets advises us to go see Monument Park first before the game starts and we do. It was someting to see! I'm not a Yankees fan but as a baseball fan, Monument Park is pretty special. To see all of that Yankee history, I sensed that it was a preview of what we would see on the next stop of our journey in Cooperstown.

Tate and Trey in front of New Yankee Stadium

We found our seats for the game in the upper deck behind the 3rd base line. The boys and I were in awe. It was a good game. Hiroki Kuroda started for the Yankees and Mark Buerhle started for the Toronto Blue Jays. It was also a special treat for the boys to get to see Derek Jeter who was playing his last season. He began with the Yankees in 1995. Tammy and I are seeing the Yankees in New York for the second time. The first time was back in 2004 when we saw Jeter's iconic play where he dove into the stands going after a foul ball against the Red Sox at the old Yankee Stadium. Jeter suffered a broken nose.
In this game four home runs were hit; two by former Hickory Crawdad Jose Bautista, one by Carlos Beltran (a favorite player of

Trey's), and one by Ichiro Suzuki, his first of the season and the game winner. The Yanks won 6-4. After the game we got back on the subway and returned to Port Authority where we cught the bus back to our hotel. It was a very long day but one where a lot of memories were made. Time to rest up for the drive to Cooperstown the next day and for me, the highlight of the trip.

Yankee Stadium Jumbotron. Monument Park is located below and behind the centerfield wall.

A Panoramic view from our seats. It is a beautiful stadium.

CHAPTER 5 - COOPERSTOWN AND THE HALL OF FAME

Oh man!, the day I had been looking forward to for 5 years had arrived. That's when Greg Maddux and Tom Glavine retired from playing baseball. I had watched those guys during the glory days when Atlanta won 14 straight division titles. I knew these guys would be first ballot Hall of Famers and the sports writers made it official this past winter that they were going into the Hall of Fame. And to make it better, Bobby Cox was also going in with Joe Torre and Tony La Russa. Frank Thomas, one of the most feared hitters of all time, was also going to be enshrined. If there was ever a time to go to an induction, this would be it. Again, I have to give Tammy credit. She was determined to make it happen that we get there. And we did, we were going to Cooperstown, although we had to get a room that was 40 miles away (Tammy booked it 4 months ago!). Apparently this was the same story for a lot of people. There are very few hotels there and the ones they do have are booked up years in advance on Hall of Fame weekend.

We arrive on Saturday afternoon and begin our stroll through the streets of Cooperstown. It is a quaint little town nestled in the hills of upstate western New York. You don't just happen by it. But it is like stepping back in time. It is a carnival-like atmosphere this weekend. There are former players signing autographs at tables on the street (for a small fee which I didn't like but that was the only way to keep order I guess). We saw former Braves John Smoltz, John Rocker, Ryan Klesko, and

Marquis Grissom signing anything people would give them. Pete Rose was also rumored to be in town but we didn't see him.

Then we prepare to witness one of the best kept secrets in all of baseball: the Hall of Famers Parade. At least I did not know of it. But every Hall of Fame Weekend on Saturday at 6:00 the returning Hall of Famers participate in a parade where each player and his spouse or other family member ride in the back of a pickup truck right through the middle of town. This is a chance for the fans to get up close to see some of baseball's living legends. It was unbelievable. There we were just a few yards away from some of the greats of all time. We pushed our way as close as we could to try to get a front row seat. We pushed the boys up to be right along the rail to get a good view. No thanks to this guy from Chicago who as Tammy put it, was not "kid minded".

Here is a short list of some of the players we saw: Hank Aaron, Whitey Ford, Ernie Banks, Phil Neikro, Gaylord Perry, Mike Schmidt, George Brett, Johnny Bench, Cal Ripken, Reggie Jackson, Tom Seaver, Tommy Lasorda, Carlton Fisk, Bob Gibson, Lou Brock, Ricky Henderson, and Barry Larkin just to name a few. Over 50 players returned to honor the new inductees who were at the end of the parade. Finally, the "new guys" came through in alphabetical order so as not to favor one over the other: Bobby Cox, Tom Glavine, Tony La Russa, Greg Maddux, Frank Thomas, and Joe Torre.

New Inductee Greg Maddux in the Hall of Famer Parade

The parade was probably the biggest highlight of the trip for me. It was like a dream. Every baseball fan needs to experience that. I'm sure the grin stayed on my face for hours afterwards. Could it get any better?

We drive the 45 minutes back to Norwich where our room is and spend the night only to drive back the next morning for the next day's events. After finally getting a parking place we walked through Cooperstown to the Hall of Fame. Again, on the way, there are more signings going on at different places. We saw Darryl Strawberry and Dale Murphy among others. We stand in line to get into the Museum for about 30 minutes. We finally get in and see the exhibits for about 45 minutes when we have to leave to catch the shuttle out to where the induction ceremony will be held which is about a mile away. We arrived at this field which reminded me of what Woodstock must have been like. As I found out later, there were approximately 48,000 people there to see the ceremony. Of course we were not even close to the stage. In fact, we must have been 5-6 hundred yards away. Fortunately they had a big jumbotron screen and adequate speakers to allow us to view the ceremony. Another indication of how large the crowd was could be seen by the fact that there were well over 100 porta johns there too.

The Major League Baseball Hall of Fame in Cooperstown, NY

The ceremony began and good thing for us the three Braves inductees went first. No disrespect to the other guys but we were ready to leave at that point as the boys were getting hot. For me, the speeches were great. Very meaningful and moving. I have never been more proud to be a Braves fan. It was an awesome event. After Bobby Cox spoke we decided to head back into town and finish our tour of the Hall of Fame. The boys were exhausted and did not really appreciate all the baseball history that they were exposed to but I think it will be memorable nonetheless. The amount of baseball memorabilia in the Hall of Fame is overwhelming. One can not do it justice in one afternoon. So we picked out what I thought should be the highlights for the boys and made our way through the exhibits. We had had our fill of baseball nostalgia and headed out of town. I remember thinking as we left what an overwhelming couple of days we had just enjoyed. It would take a while for all of it to really set in. Like I said, this was going to be the highlight of the trip, or so I thought.

Our view of the Hall of Fame Induction Ceremony

After an unforgettable day full of baseball history, we left Cooperstown and headed 280 miles east to Boston.

Postscript - The boys and I would go back to Cooperstown in 2019. Tate was invited to play with a team when he was 12 at Cooperstown Dreams Park which is where thousands of young boys go each summer to play for a week. Trey would go with us and we would get a chance to revisit the Hall of Fame. It is such a beautiful place. I don't know if I could ever get tired of going there.

Tate (pictured below at age 12) actually got invited to play at the Cooperstown Dreams Park for a week in 2019 and we were able to go back . I highly recommend to any 12 year-old to go there and play. It was awesome experience!

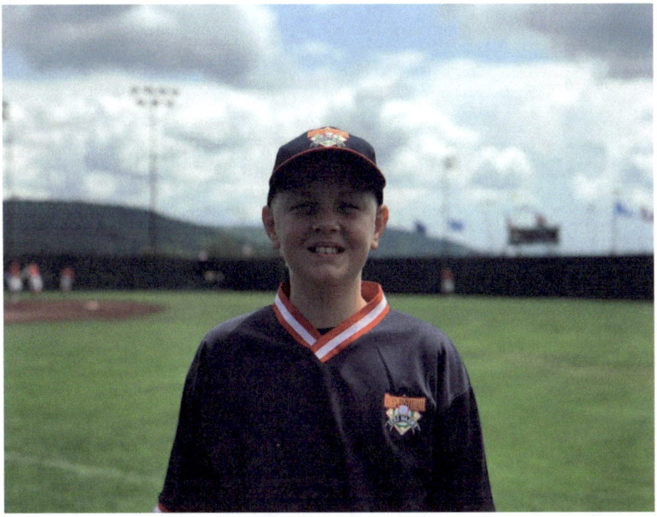

CHAPTER 6 - BOSTON #4 FENWAY PARK! SO GOOD, SO GOOD, SO GOOD!

This game was one that I, and we as a family, had really been looking forward to. My youngest, Tate, had become a big Red Sox fan when he learned that they were his cousin, JR's favorite team. And I have always wanted to go to the famous Fenway Park. This was going to be a treat. We stayed the night in the town of Waltham which is just west of Boston. Since it was day 6, we were desperately needing to do some laundry so Tammy decided to go get that taken care of (I did volunteer to do it but I guess she wanted it done right) while I entertained the kids in the indoor pool. It was nice to get to enjoy a leisurely morning. Afterwards we find a Moe's Southwestern Grill nearby for lunch and then head into the city via the light rail.

We arrive in the city and make the short walk to Yawkey Way. We get our tickets and then hit the stores looking for Red Sox souvenirs. By this time it is nearly 4:30 and the gates don't open until 5:20 so we go to a place called Loretta's for supper. This was chosen because it offered southern country cooking and country music as its theme. By now during the trip I needed a little taste of southern atmosphere.

The view of Yawkey War outside Fenway Park

We finish eating and head across the street to the stadium. The boys and I were giddy with anticipation of what it might be like inside the 100 year old iconic ballpark. It is very difficult to describe it. Simply amazing. Again, I felt like I had stepped back in time. It just had that nostalgic feeling of a different era. The park had the smells of great food and all the vendors selling various items like you would see at any stadium but it just had a different feel to it. It was incredible. We made our way to our seats which were located in the lower level very close to the right field foul pole that every true baseball fan knows as "Pesky's Pole" named for Johnny Pesky who played for Boston in the 40s and 50s. Immediately the boys are awed by the sights of The Green Monster, Boston's famous 37 feet high left field wall. Trey had even gotten a Green Monster T-shirt before we went inside the stadium. We had great seats for a matchup between the Sox with Clay Bucholz as the starter and the Toronto Blue Jays. I wasn't really excited about seeing the Blue Jays again but after finding out that R.A. Dickey, the famous knuckleballer and former Cy Young Award winner was the starter, the boys and I were pumped. As a bonus we got to see Dickey warm up in right field directly in front of us. It was fun for the boys and me to see his knuckleball in action up close.

The view from our seats with the Green Monster in the background

Unfortunately for Tate, the game was not even close. R.A. had the Boston hitters off balance all night. He was sharp, even striking out David Ortiz (Tate's favorite player and Boston's most feared hitter) twice. The Blue Jays jumped out to an early lead thanks to a Melky Cabrera home run over the "Green Monster", which was pretty exciting for the boys to see. The final score was

14-1. Tate was a little bummed out but was not surprised since the Red Sox had been struggling all year. The outcome of the game was not a big deal. The fact that we were at Fenway Park was all that mattered and to see the permanent grin on Tate's face was priceless. The highlight of the experience was probably hearing all those Boston fans singing Neil Diamond's "Sweet Caroline" in the 8th inning, which is why I titled this chapter the way I did. Everything about the experience at Fenway was "So Good"!

I think we were all in agreement that this was our favorite park that we had visited up to this point. Another amazing experience on what had become a most incredible journey.

Tate standing in front of Pesky's Pole

CHAPTER 7 - BACK TO NYC #5 NEW YORK METS' CITIFIELD

Day seven (Tuesday) began with us leaving Boston and deliberating whether or not we wanted to go back into New York City. Tammy and I had kind of decided to skip the Mets game as we really didn't want to deal with the city again. But after much consideration on my part, I suggested that we go ahead and do it. After all, we had become experienced travelers and since we had done it one time, it wouldn't be that bad. Besides, we would probably be really upset if we fulfilled this dream of attending all the Major League parks and we had to go back to New York to cover the Mets. "We are right here. Let's do it!"

We headed back into the city on I-95 and drove over the George Washington bridge, which was pretty neat. We reserved a room in Secaucus, NJ near the place we had stayed a few nights earlier. It was mid afternoon when we arrived so we decided to start heading into NYC. We head to the bus stop and get our bus passes and prepare for the 15 minute ride to the Port Authority station in Manhattan. As the bus arrives, the driver notifies us that the air conditioning was not working. "No problem", we say. It won't be that long of a ride. Little did we know that it was now 5:00 and traffic into the city was at a stand still. This turned into the MOST MISERABLE ride of my life. On a ride that was probably 5 miles in distance, it took us 2 HOURS to get there on a bus that had no AC. The only relief we had was the roof vent at the top of the bus. It was HORRIBLE. I have to commend the boys. They did great and did not complain too much. Needless to say, we took the first opportunity to get off the "bus ride from Hell" after we exited the Lincoln Tunnel. It was now after 7:00 and the game was to begin at 7:05.

We arrive at Port Authority and head for the subway for a ride into Queens. Here is where another valuable lesson was learned. It turned out we were not as experienced as we thought. When going a great distance across town, take the express line! We took the number 7 local train which had to make 19 stops before we could reach Queens and the Mets Stadium - Citi Field. It took a while. I did not know much about Queens, but found out that it is a pretty big borough. Most of what I had in mind was learned by watching "The King of Queens" on TV. No surprise, it wasn't much like that at all. Finally, we arrive and head to the ticket counter. We had missed three innings already so we just got 4 seats in the upper deck and headed inside.

Panoramic view of CitiField - Home of the New York Mets

Wow! What a beautiful ballpark! Nestled deep inside one of the least aesthetically pleasing boroughs in NYC is this jewel of a stadium. It was very impressive. The Mets were playing the Phillies and by the time we got to our seats the game was in the 4th inning with the Phillies winning 2-0. Cole Hamels was pitching again for the Phillies (who we saw pitch against the Giants back in Philly). Dillon Gee was on the mound for the Mets. The highlight of the game came in the 7th inning when

Phillies second baseman Chase Utley hit a Grand Slam to right field making the final score 6-0. After the game, we caught the No. 7 Express back to the other side of NYC (It didn't take nearly as long to get back, thus the name express!). I regret that we did not get to see much of CiitField. I would have liked to seen more of it as i don't think we really got ot enjoy it. Maybe we can get back there someday.

We were finally through with NYC although it was bittersweet to look back across the Hudson River as we exited the Lincoln Tunnel on the New Jersey side to see the beautiful New York City skyline and be in awe of how the city looks at night. Another park checked off and another day down. The next day we would head south into Baltimore.

CHAPTER 8 - BALTIMORE AND #6 CAMDEN YARDS

Wednesday July 30 - As we left New Jersey, we were thinking about not making the trip to Washington to watch the Nationals. We had been going hard for a week now and we were getting tired and missing our own more comfortable beds. Tammy and I had decided that Baltimore would be our last stop on this trip and surprisingly, the boys were okay with that. We had rationalized the decision by saying that Washington would be a whole other trip and we could just include a visit to Nationals Park when we come back to see the Nation's capital later when the boys would be older and could appreciate it more. That decision would work out very well as we would do a D.C. trip in 2018 when the All-Star game is held there.

Trey had been looking forward to this stop as the Orioles are probably his second favorite team (after the Braves). His favorite player is third baseman Manny Machado who plays for the Orioles. As an added bonus, the O's were playing the Los Angeles Angels who have one of the most exciting teams in baseball with players like Mike Trout, Albert Pujols, and Josh Hamilton.

Tate in the shade of the Cal Ripken monument waiting for the gates to open

We arrive in Baltimore around 3:00 in the afternoon and we check into our hotel and then order our tickets over the phone. Since it was a weekday game, good seats were readily available. Our hotel was within walking distance to Camden Yards so we got there around 4:30 and did a little souvenir shopping. The gates opened at 5:05 and we wanted to get inside to watch batting practice and hopefully catch a ball or get an autograph. When the gates opened we entered Eutaw Way and headed for the outfield bleachers where we saw the Orioles taking batting practice. We went down to the front row and admired all of the hits and the boys begged the Oriole players for a ball like everyone else. Trey's favorite player just happened to be taking BP and I was hoping he could hit one our way. Wouldn't you know it, we were not there long when Manny Machado hits a shot to deep center field where we were standing. It didn't make it over the fence but hit the warning track and bounced right over Trey and Tate's heads and right into my hand. Score!! I had snagged a ball for the boys that was hit by Trey's favorite player. My ticket to be "Dad of the Year" was punched! Trey has been enamored with that ball ever since.

After batting practice we headed to our seats, which were down the third base line about 10 rows back. Really good seats for $30. Tammy and Trey went and got us something to eat from Boog's BBQ named for Baltimore icon Boog Powell. It was pretty tasty. The game was very entertaining. Baltimore started the scoring early in the first inning when a Manny Machado single was followed by an Adam Jones home run. Baltimore's starting pitcher, Kevin Gausman had a perfect game through 5 innings. The Angels' big three went 1-12 in the game and did not have much of an impact. The Orioles won the game 4-3.

Orioles Park at Camden Yards is a beautiful stadium. The atmosphere and the fans are very friendly. Outside of Fenway Park, I think that Orioles Park was probably my second favorite ballpark (Sorry NY). It was kind of a depressing feeling to think that this would be it for baseball games for a while, but we were anxious to get back home. After the game, we walked back to the hotel which was about 2 blocks away. The next day we were going home.

The Scoreboard at Camden Yards

Trey and "Crazy Hair" Tate outside Camden Yards

CHAPTER 9 - FINALLY, HOME, SWEET HOME! - YEAR ONE COMPLETE

Thursday July 31st, 2014 - We left the hotel around 9:30 am and headed out of town, not before I could get a short little history field trip in. I just had to go out and see Fort McHenry, site of the famous War of 1812 battle where the British were turned back in September, 1814. It was also the place where Francis Scott Key witnessed the "broad stripes and bright stars" through "the dawn's early light". Yes, where the Star Spangled Banner was written. It was a nice little field trip. Even the boys thought it was interesting. Tammy was ready to get home and we got out of there around 12.

While on the 6 hour drive home, we were able to sit back and try to get an appreciation for everything that we had done in the past week. What an unbelievable adventure. We had seen 5 ball games in 5 different parks in an eight day span. Also sandwiched in between was a two day stop in Cooperstown for Hall of Fame weekend. That in itself would have been a great trip, but to do all the other things that we had done on this trip made this one amazing journey.

I don't know that Trey and Tate can fully appreciate all that they got to see and do yet. Probably not for a while, and that's okay, but they can at least say that they have been to those places. After 2215 miles of riding in a car, 8 nights of staying in hotels, over 10 days of eating meals that were not home-cooked, 5 baseball stadiums and games, we can all look back and enjoy the incredible memories that were made.

We got home around 8:30 on Thursday the 31st after leaving out on Wednesday the 23rd of July and we were glad to get home. A big "thank you" to my mother-in-law for house sitting and taking care of our dog. And a big "thank you" to Tammy for being such a great spouse and mom for putting this entire trip together. Without her, it would not have happened. She is the best!

I can't wait to take another trip next year!

CHAPTER 10 - 2015 - #7 GREAT AMERICAN BALLPARK - CINCINNATI

Here we go again! Baseball Trip 2015 - Jensen Family Baseball Excursion Part Deux (Yes, French for a reason) After the success of last year's trip covering the Northeast, we decided to give it a go one more time to see if we could continue this quest to see all 30 Major League stadiums before our sons graduate from high school. This year we would be doing what I will call the "Rust Belt" Tour which consists of the cities of Cincinnati, Detroit, Toronto, Cleveland, and Pittsburgh. Now, you may be wondering what that term "Rust Belt" really means but it refers to the industrialized areas and factory cities that have felt the hard times of a suffering economy impacted by recession and increased competition from overseas that has forced some factories to close down and no longer be used.

Once again my lovely wife Tammy and I researched the MLB schedule to try to find dates that would work when the aforementioned teams would be playing at home. We knew there would be side field trips that we would need to take along the way so we decided that the two weeks around the 4th of July would work out the best. We headed out on June 29th headed north.

We left on the morning of the 29th headed for Cincinnati where we would watch the Reds take on the Minnesota Twins that night at The Great American Ballpark. Our first side trip would take place in Louisville where we drove maybe an hour out of the way to see the Louisville Slugger Bat Factory. We've got to go there while on a baseball trip, right? Well worth the trip. We got to see the world's largest bat as well as see all the famous signatures that have been on the Louisville Slugger bats. There were also batting cages where we got to try out some wooden bats. I chose the bat size used by Hank Aaron and I'll have to say I did quite well albeit the pitches were only about 65 mph and were at a consistent speed.

Trey and Tate outside the Louiville Slugger Bat Company

From there it was on to Cincinnati. Now this year, unlike

last year, we decided to plan ahead. Although it was fun and adventurous not to have any reservations or tickets last year, I don't think my nerves could take it this year (and neither could Tammy's I don't think). And since it was going to take place around the 4th of July holiday, we decided to make reservations and book our tickets online ahead of time. I'm glad we did. It made the trip much more enjoyable. Here is where I need to get a plug in. Our two sights that helped us out tremendously were hotels.com and tickpick.com. There is also another site that Tammy discovered called ballparkchasers.com that have given us lots of advice on places to stay and things to do in the areas. Apparently what we are doing is really a thing that lots of people do. Who knew?

I was really looking forward to our first stop. The Great American Ballpark, home of this year's 2015 Major League Baseball All-Star Game. The city was buzzing with anticipation and everything was in tip-top shape as the game was only a couple of weeks away. We stayed across the River in Belleview, Kentucky and took a local trolley across the bridge that crosses the Ohio River into Cincinnati. The Ballpark is magnificent. It reminds me of the throwback styles of stadiums where there is not a bad seat anywhere. I was able to find us seats in the upper deck in the front row for $11 each. Not bad since they were below face value. Tammy had created a budget for this trip. Like I mentioned earlier, she is a planner and had set a specific amount that I could spend when shopping for tickets. Her budgeted amount for tickets was $20 per person which as any baseball fan knows is not much to get good seats so I sacrificed a little on this one so I could pay a little more for seats later on. But as we sat down in our seats we could see everything very well.

Our view of the field. Notice the Ohio River in the background

The game was very entertaining and the Reds ended up winning 11-7. The highlight was at the end when we got to see arguably the most exciting pitcher in the game, Aroldis Chapman, pitch the 9th inning. It was pretty amazing to get to see someone who throws 103 mph. at the conclusion of the 8th inning, we moved down to the lower level to and stood in SRO (standing room only) areas to get a better look at Chapman as he pitched. We had a good view of the batters and felt sorry for them trying to hit 100+ mph! Electric stuff!

After the game we made our way back to our hotel. We decided to walk across the bridge that spans the Ohio River. A local told us we could make it in "maybe 10 minutes". As we were walking across the bridge, the History teacher in me could not help but think about what it must have been like over 165 years ago when this exact spot was the last stop for escaped slaves on the Underground Railroad. Cincinnati came to represent the land of freedom as the Ohio River also marked the boundary between the North and the South. Nearly 30 minutes later we arrived at our hotel. One ballpark down. The next day we would head to Detroit.

Trey and Tate outside Great American BallPark

Trey sporting his new Todd Frazier T-shirt

CHAPTER 11 - STADIUM #8 COMERICA PARK - DETROIT

Days 2 & 3, from the Queen City to the Motor City. On Tuesday, June 30, we headed north up through western Ohio headed to Detroit, Michigan. This was the stop that I was a little nervous about considering the not-so-great, sketchy reputation that Detroit has. We booked a room in Dearborn, MI which is just outside of Detroit. After finding our hotel and checking in, we made our way to Comerica Park to see the Tigers host the Pittsburgh Pirates. We decided ahead of time to park as close to the stadium as we could so we wouldn't have a long walk back to the car after the night game. And after driving through Detroit in the daytime, I sure didn't want to have to walk in certain parts of downtown at night.

We arrived at the stadium and parked right next to Ford Field which is where the Detroit Lions play and is right beside Comerica Park. It was a 2 minute walk to the stadium so I was ok. When we got inside, "oh my!". What a beautiful ballpark. It was a very nice stadium, full of rich Detroit Tiger history. After all the negative things I had heard about Detroit, I was surprised to see such a nice facility. The boys were excited because we would get to see Tiger greats Miguel Cabrera, Yoenis Cespedis, and Justin Verlander, the starting pitcher for the Tigers. They were playing the Pirates who featured some former Hickory Crawdad players like Andrew McCutcheon and Neil Walker. The game turned out to be very entertaining with J.D. Martinez hitting a home run to tie the game and sending it to extra innings. Now extra innings is usually pretty exciting for me because it means free baseball, but after a long day of driving and stressing out about being in Detroit, my family was very tired so we only made it through the 10th inning before we decided to leave. We did listen to some of it on the radio as we were leaving but we were already back at the hotel and in bed before the game ended. It turned out that the game went fourteen innings with the Pirates winning.

Trey and Tate at Comerica Park - Detroit

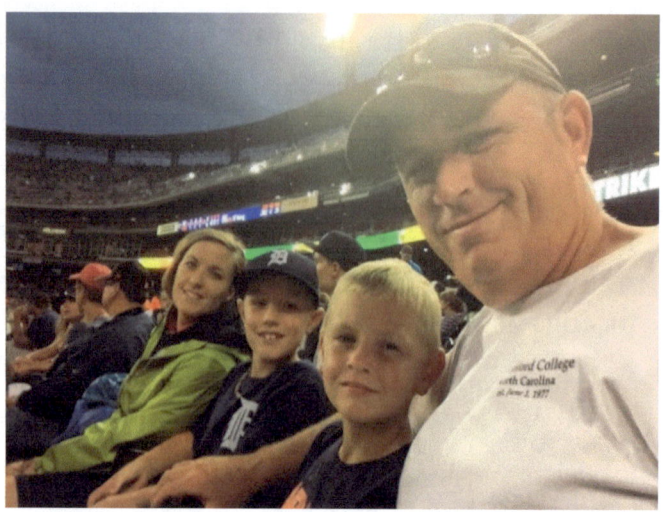

Family pic from our seats - the boys sporting Tiger Tees

The next day was going to be another one of Dad's history field trips. While doing research about Detroit, I read a lot about the Henry Ford Museum and the many other attractions associated with it. As an American History teacher and a parent, I just had to take the family to see it.

Henry Ford was also a big fan of American History and went to great lengths to try to preserve it. So he created Greenfield Village, which is an attraction where visitors feel like they have gone back in time to see actual historic sights and homeplaces.

The boys at the Liberty Craftworks section of Greenfield Village

For example, we saw a working farm where Harvey Firestone, the great tire king, grew up. We also saw working craft shops where potters, weavers, and glass blowers were doing things that were done over 200 years ago. We saw the home places of Noah Webster, George Washington Carver, and the Wright Brothers. There was a one room schoolhouse where William McGuffey actually taught using his famous McGuffey Reader.

Tate conducting class in the McGuffey one-room schoolhouse

There were several exhibits showcasing the workshops of Thomas Edison. And of course we saw an exhibit that showcased Henry Ford's workshop where he created his famous automobiles. The highlight for all of us was to actually take a ride in a Model T.

After Greenfield Village, we went to the Henry Ford Museum where there were all kinds of exhibits showcasing different modes of transportation. There were cars of every decade, tractors, buses, and airplanes. There were Presidential limousines and the actual bus that Rosa Parks refused to give up her seat in which arguably began the Civil Rights Movement of the 1950s. Below are some of the more interesting exhibits that could be seen.

Tate in the seat that Rosa Parks refused to give up.

The bus where it all began in Montgomery, Alabama

You'll notice that Tate seems to be in most of these pictures. He is my little history fan and stuck right with me while we were checking out the exhibits. Trey and Tammy had already had enough and were maxed out on historical stuff. I had gotten my history fix for the day and we left. We decided to go to Red Robin for dinner and then back to the hotel to get ready for our trip into Canada the next day!

CHAPTER 12 - STADIUM #9 - ROGERS CENTRE - TORONTO

After two days in the Detroit area and the stress of being there, I was really looking forward to going to Toronto. Not far from Detroit, you cross over into Canada via the Ambassador Bridge. This was the part of the trip that was the most involved during preparations as we all had to have a passport to be able to cross the border. That in itself was a big hassle. We kind of waited around to the last minute about a month ago to try to get our passports but they finally arrived two days before we left home to start this trip. But we had the necessary documentation so crossing into Canada was a breeze, thankfully.

It was neat for the boys to be able to say they have been in another country and I have to say, after being in Detroit, going to Ontario, Canada was truly a breath of fresh air. I have grown to really like Canada. Canada is a really NICE place. The people are very friendly and polite. They go to great lengths to emphasize cleanliness, recycling, and preserving natural resources. It is a very progressive-minded nation, at least in my opinion. Sure you have to get used to everything being printed in two languages (English and French) and the whole metric system thing which makes it kind of confusing when you are dealing with kilometers and liters instead of miles and gallons. The speed limit on the highways was 100 km/h. I couldn't help but notice the irony as we crossed over the Ambassador Bridge from a very run down, dilapidated, dirty Detroit into

Windsor, Ontario how different things were. It was like going to a whole different world. As we proceeded onto the QEW (Queen Elizabeth Way), we were traveling through lush, green farmlands. It was as if there were no people for miles, which I knew was not true, but I think the Canadian government, or maybe it is the Province of Ontario, have gone to great lengths not to "clutter up" their highways and exits. You don't see the fast food restaurants, hotels, shopping centers, and gas stations like you see at every exit in the US. Everything is much more aesthetically pleasing in Canada. It was that way for three hours as we approached the city of Toronto when things started to get a little more urbanized. It was also on that stretch of road where I got my first taste of Poutine at a restaurant when we stopped for lunch. Yes, you read that right, Poutine, which is pronounced like routine, is a very popular Canadian dish and it is nothing more than cheese curds piled over French Fries and smothered in brown gravy. Delicious!

Toronto is located right on Lake Ontario. It is an older looking city with tall buildings covered in glass and there is the famous CN Tower which stands out above the skyline. You can go up in the 1800 foot tower for a hefty price which a few Canucks (Canadians) said really wasn't worth what they charged. We found our hotel which was only two blocks from the Rogers Centre, home of the Toronto Blue Jays, and we checked in. After a quick rest, we made our way to the game. Again as we walked, I couldn't help but notice how clean the city was and how nice all the people were. When we got inside, there was an air of excitement as most of the people there were very excited about their team and then I realized, Toronto is the only MLB team in Canada so the Blue Jays truly are a National Team.

Our first stadium with a retractable roof. A beautiful ballpark.

The game featured the Blue Jays hosting the Boston Red Sox. This was a special treat for Tate, as he is kind of a big Red Sox fan. The game got out of hand very quickly as the Red Sox scored 7 runs before ever recording an out in the 1st inning, a deficit which the Blue Jays never recovered from, although they did score 4 in the second inning. Tate got to see his favorite player, David Ortiz hit a home run, so he was excited. The Red Sox won easily and as Tate pointed out it was a little payback since we saw Toronto blow out Boston at Fenway last year (I had forgotten that). But all in all we enjoyed the game. Trey really liked the Rogers Centre and has put it in his top 5 list.

Trey and Tate from our seats in the first row of the upper deck. Tate is tired of posing

After the game, we head back to the hotel for a late night swim at the indoor pool and turn in. Stadium number 9 is in the books. The next day we would head back south to Niagara Falls. This was going to be a stop we were all looking forward to.

CHAPTER 13 - NIAGARA FALLS!

After spending one night in Toronto, we decided we would take a little break from baseball and just enjoy the sites in Canada. What better place to do that than in Niagara Falls. Tammy and I had both been there before but I was really excited for the boys to be able to see how marvelous it really is. What a breathtaking place! It is very difficult to describe.

I'm not sure if it is one of the "Great Wonders of the World", but it is definitely one of the great "Wonders of North America" in my opinion. We decided that if we are going to see it, then we are going to do it right. We went ahead and bought the Niagara Falls Adventure Pass which enabled us to ride "The Hornblower", which is Canada's version of the Maid in the Mist; a boat ride on the Niagara River right up to where the water comes crashing over the falls. This is where everyone is given a lovely red poncho to wear to keep from getting wet. But it is really the best way to see the falls!

What an amazing, breath-taking experience. The pictures really to not do it justice. We also were able to view a short IMAX type movie that involved some really cool special effects that talked about the history of the falls. We had a great day at the falls and returned to our hotel.

We stayed at the Americana Resort, Spa, and Waterpark, which was a hotel that had an actual water park inside it. Tammy really out-did herself on this hotel because if anything could trump Niagara Falls, (according to Tate anyway) this place was it! This might have been Tate's favorite part of the whole trip because everywhere we went after Niagara, Tate wanted us to find another water park to go to. It really was a lot of fun, and it allowed the boys to exert some energy.

It was very difficult for us to leave Niagara Falls but we were ready to get back to the "good ole USA" and resume our journey. We came back across the border on Saturday, the 4th of July and headed toward Erie, PA which is where we stopped for the night on our way to Cleveland.

We had decided to try to find a fireworks show to see on Lake Erie so we headed to a State Park right on the lake to get a good view.

We found an open field at the park where the boys could play some wiffle ball.

After time at the State Park we decided to get some dinner and return to our hotel. We were so tired that we didn't make it to the fireworks. We just watched the Macy's Fireworks show on TV. The next day we would head to Cleveland.

CHAPTER 14 - CLEVELAND ROCKS! - #10 PROGRESSIVE FIELD

Sunday July 5th was another travel day and I was thinking of Kenny Chesney's song, "Anything But Mine", and the lyrics, "In the morning I'm leaving making my way back to Cleveland", we headed southwest toward the city. We did not have tickets for a baseball game until Monday night in Cleveland so we had a little time to kill which for us means we try to find some outlets to keep Mom happy. Tammy found some just 20 miles southeast of the city and we spent most of the early afternoon there before driving on into the city.

We get into Cleveland around 2:30 in the afternoon which leaves me just enough time to go and check out one of Cleveland's main attractions, the Rock 'n Roll Hall of Fame. Tammy and the boys were not really interested which meant I would have to (get to) go by myself. It was only a 15 minute walk so off I went while my family stayed back at the hotel.

It was a real treat for me. Unfortunately they closed at 5:30 which meant I only had a couple of hours. The Hall of Fame and the exhibits were really cool. Two hours was just not enough time but I saw what I could.

The Hall of Fame is a beautiful building that sits right by Lake Erie.

One of Elvis' outfits he wore in his early years (had to take this pic for Tate"s teacher, Miss Bliss, since Elvis was one of her favorites).

Drum set used by Ringo Starr of The Beatles.

There was lots of great stuff in there and anyone who loves music and history should go visit this attraction if ever in Cleveland.

I made it back to the room and we went to a local pub called Flannery's where we had dinner and watched the beginning of the Women's World Cup Soccer Final. The game was awesome as they jumped all over Japan early. Afterwards we headed back to the hotel for the night.

The next day we needed to get some laundry done so we found a place that did it for $.85 per pound and dropped it off. There were lots of stores nearby so we did some more shopping before grabbing lunch and heading back to the room to get ready to go to the game.

On this trip we had made it a priority to get to the stadiums right when they opened to try to get a ball during batting practice. So far we had been shut out. So I asked Trey if he had a good feeling about this one before going in and he said yes. After reading some tips online about how to get a ball, when the gates opened at 5, we were ready. I have to give props to Progressive Field in Cleveland. They are very "fan friendly ". They open the gates 2 hours before game time whereas most places open an hour early.

Why does it matter? You get to see the home team bat as well as the visitors which means double the chance to get a ball! I had also read that if you are first in line, you should sprint to the right field section that is open. You could probably just pick one up in the bleachers since no one was there yet. Well, that is what we did and wouldn't you know it, I found one on the back row as others were charging to the front. I also read that you could possibly find a ball in the bushes of Heritage Park. That is a garden in the centerfield section of the outfield that honors all the Cleveland Indians' great players. As we were looking at the monuments we happened to find another ball behind the fence in some shrubbery. Another score! All total, we left with 4 balls retrieved from batting practice. Mission accomplished!

The game featured the Indians hosting the Houston Astros which was a treat for me since the Astros are one of the best teams and best stories in baseball right now.

As I said, Progressive Field is one of the most Fan Friendly parks that we have been to. There is so much for the kids to do to keep them entertained and they have some of the best prices on concessions than anywhere else we had been. I especially got a kick out of a particular stand called Dad's Place that sold some low end beer (Natural Light, Schlitz, PBR, etc.) for $4 a can which was cheap by ballpark standards.

The game was very entertaining with the Astros winning 9-4.

A panoramic view of our seats at Progressive Field.

Tribe Town - Cleveland Scoreboard

After the game we headed back to the room for the night. The next morning we had to swing by and pick up our laundry and there was one more little side trip that I wanted to make. About a half mile from the laundromat was 55th Street which may be better known by some Holiday movie lovers as Cleveland Street. That's right, the actual house used in my all-time favorite Christmas movie, "A Christmas Story".

The boys and I on the porch of the Christmas Story House!

"A Christmas Story" is the iconic classic that came out in the early 80s. You know, the one with the line, "you'll shoot your eye out, kid". Here is the actual house that was used in the movie. I just had to go see it. Tammy, who does not appreciate quality films like I do, was nice enough to indulge me on this one. There was even a leg lamp in the window!

I could just hear Ralphie's "Old Man" saying, "You should see how it looks from out here!"

What a great attraction and a fortuitous find on our journey! There was even a gift shop with all kinds of novelties tied to the movie. I really got a kick out of that place. But it was back in the van and we were on our way to our last stop, Pittsburgh.

CHAPTER 15 - "THE STEEL CITY" - #11 - PITTSBURGH'S PNC PARK

After nearly taking a full lap around Lake Erie in the last week it was now time for us to head southeast to Pittsburgh and the last stop on this trip. This is the stadium that I had been looking forward to the most as I had heard many great things about PNC Park. So on Tuesday morning we left Cleveland and made the 2+ hour drive to the "Steel City". We arrived at our hotel in the early afternoon. Unfortunately we did not get a hotel that was within walking distance, but the Holiday Inn Express did have a shuttle service that could get us to a subway station which they call the "T" that would take us to the stadium. Now I have to give a little credit to the city of Pittsburgh. They have a toll free zone that is within the downtown district. Amazingly, anyone can ride the subway and not have to pay a toll for any stops within that district which includes about 8 or 10 stops which gets us to the stadium. So that was nice. I intentionally took one stop before the stop at Allegheny station because I wanted us to experience walking to PNC Park across the iconic and picturesque Roberto Clemente Bridge which can be seen beyond the outfield of PNC Park and honors the legacy of one of the best players to ever play the game.

Tate and Trey posing in the middle of Roberto Clemente Bridge

This was a great time to tell the family about Roberto Clemente. He is still considered an icon in Pittsburgh and is still hailed as one of the all time greats. So tragic that his life was cut short in a plane crash while he was helping deliver supplies to earthquake victims in Nicaragua in 1972.

The boys in front of the Roberto Clemente Statue

We arrived at the ballpark early to get ready to see the Pirates host the San Diego Padres. We walked through Riverfront Way which is a section right along the river where vendors are selling all sorts of food and souvenirs. This is where Trey gets his last t-shirt on this trip, a Pirates one with Andrew McCutcheon's name on the back. Then we head inside to try to get another batting practice ball to add to the collection. When we get in, the Padres are taking batting practice. Now, as a Braves fan, it was difficult for me to watch as there were three former Braves on the field (2 of whom I wish were still in Atlanta). And to rub salt into the wound, Justin Upton, one of the players I would like for the Braves to still have, was putting on a show hitting tape measure home runs into the second deck over our heads rattling the seats. It was quite impressive. We also saw Craig Kimbrel, the most dominant closer in the game when he was in Atlanta, running around in the outfield shagging balls for the Padres.

The boys and I watching BP, hoping to catch a ball.

Well, wouldn't you know it? As we scattered out in a short radius to try to increase our chances of getting a ball, a little while later Tate comes running back with a ball in hand. Apparently some older guy gave it to him. Who could resist not giving up a ball to that cute little guy!

After BP was over, we got some food and made it to our seats. We were on the 7th row on the first base side just beyond the Padres dugout. The seats were great!

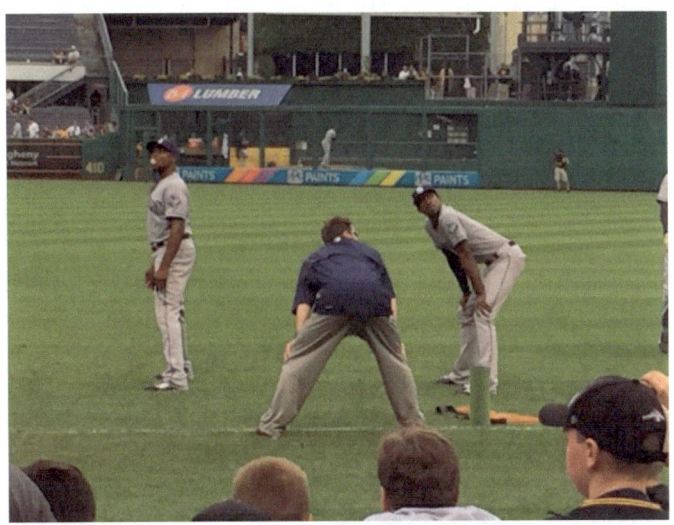

The Upton Brothers, Justin and BJ, stretching before the game.

The seats were so close to the field that the players (and especially one unsuspecting superstar named Justin Upton) were within earshot of the fans, especially one mama who was set on getting her son an autograph. Throughout the whole trip we had taken baseballs with us to get signed by a player, any player at all, with no such luck, YET. Well, as the Padre players were on the field stretching, Tammy saw an opportunity. While Trey and some other kids were gathering on the aisle next to the field, Tammy yells out in her beautiful Burke County redneck voice, "Hey Justin, can you come over here and sign a ball!?!"

Trey showing off his autographed ball signed by Justin Upton. Look at that smile!

I thought Tate was going to crawl under the seats. But it worked! Upton was kind of startled (or maybe scared, because I have heard that voice many times and it will force you to act).H He walked over with a startled grin on his face and started signing autographs, including a ball that Trey was hoping would get signed. Way to go, Mom!

Trey and Tate with the Pittsburgh Scoreboard and skyline in the distance

PNC Park is a beautiful stadium. It was built in 2001 and is part of the throw back design that resembles the parks of yesteryear. It features a wonderful view of the Pittsburgh skyline with the Clemente bridge just beyond centerfield. The field was in pristine condition. Tammy even wondered if the grass was astroturf. "No, just well manicured grass", I said. As the game started, the skies were looking rather ominous as you can tell by the pictures. And during the third inning, the bottom fell out. We had to endure an almost two hour rain delay.

Once play resumed, it was nearly 10:00 and Tammy was getting that look on her face that told me she had had enough. After 5 stadiums and 8 nights away from home and not sleeping in her own bed, I could certainly understand. So I told her that we would leave during the 7th inning stretch, which was a win for me since we had to sit through two more rain showers with ponchos on. So, I tore myself away and we headed out of the stadium to catch the subway. Right before we left our seats I remember taking one last look at the field and thinking to myself, "what a beautiful scene; to be at a Major League baseball game sitting in great seats with my family. It doesn't get much better than this".

A panoramic view from our seats

So we headed back to our hotel. This marked the last stop on year two's trip. We had seen so much in the last week and a half. The next day we would be heading home. Another great baseball adventure under our belts. 11 stadiums down with 19 more to go.

CHAPTER 16 - 2016 - #12 LOAN DEPOT PARK AND #13 TROPICANA FIELD

As we approach year three of this quest, let me recap. In 2014, we started this journey traveling to Cooperstown, NY for the Hall of Fame inductions. We decided to see as many stadiums as we could while driving to and from New York. That took us to five parks: Philadelphia, New York Yankees, Boston, New York Mets, and Baltimore. We intentionally skipped Washington as we knew we would take the boys to DC eventually someday for a big Social Studies Field Trip. Year two took us to 5 more: Cincinnati, Detroit, Toronto, Cleveland, and Pittsburgh. And if we go ahead and count Atlanta, we were at a final total of 11 Ballparks. We had covered most of the eastern United States with a couple exceptions down south in Florida.

To plan out our strategy of seeing all 30 MLB Stadiums, for us it was best to do it in chunks, or to try to cover certain regions each year like we had done in years one and two. Sometimes it works out pretty well. In other areas, it may not. So, in year 3 we decided to check off the two teams in Florida - the Marlins and the Rays. To only get two stadiums in seems a little like a waste of time and resources. So, in true Jensen fashion, we were going to make it bigger. We were going to sandwich a cruise between stadium stops!

Now the boys had never been on a cruise so this would be

something that they would really look forward to. And to make it better, we invited some familiy members to go along with us. My brother Joe and his family and Tammy's sister Lisa and her family would join us on a Carnival Cruise to the Caribbean. The boys were so excited to be going on a week-long cruise with their cousins.

For us, it was another logistical challenge, but we were used to those by now. We would go to Miami to see the Marlins, and then we would rendezvous with the family at the cruise terminal to board the ship. And then, on the way back home, we would stop in Tampa to see the Rays.

First stop - Miami. I was a little concerned about this one because I had heard Miami could be a little sketchy, but hey, we had survived Detroit so this couldn't be that bad. Surely we would be fine in Miami too. And we were. There was a lot of beautiful scenery in South Florida. Palm trees, nice beaches, and cool cars. We drove by a Lamborghini dealership and because we don't see those everyday, we just had to stop. The boys are 11 and 9 now and are just starting to have an appreciation of cool cars. And in their minds, these rank near the top as being some of the coolest!

It was "Lambo" overload and the boys were really excited!

Tate got to sit in this car with the engine running!

After spending some time dreaming about driving these unbelievable sports cars, it was back to reality and we made our way to Loan Depot Park, Home of the Miami Marlins. This was one of the newer stadiums in Major League Baseball and it had a really appealing quality in that it was enclosed, which means air conditioning! The picture below really doesn't do it justice. It was a really nice ballpark with bright colors, fairly new amenities, and did I say air conditioning? The team had not playing that well that season and on this night, they were hosting the Chicago White Sox. Not the ideal matchup, but we enjoyed the game.

A couple highlights from the game - Todd Frazier was playing for the Sox at the time and was nice enough to come over and give the boys an autograph and to interact with them some. Good dude!

Trey always enjoys getting an autograph. Thanks, Todd!

Ichiro just before he rips a double into right field

All in all, the Miami ballpark was pretty nice. It did not have the nostalgic flair that many of the older parks have, but it was a nice place to watch a game. And you could get a good seat, as demand for their tickets is not that high, unfortunately for them.

The next day we boarded the Carnival Magic to start our cruise. Rather than bore you with details about that, I will just include a couple pics:

The family had a blast but it was time to get back down to

business as we had one more stop to make before heading home.

Tampa - Tropicana Field does not get much acclaim as far as being described as a premier ballpark. It was somewhat dated as it opened up in 1990 and had some issues that needed to be addressed, but we tried to be open-minded as we went in. We were pleasantly surprised at some of the features of the building. We made our way to the park to watch the Rays as they hosted the Texas Rangers. There were some really cool features to the ballpark that made it somewhat unique.

For example, there was an aquarium with real live stingrays swimming around. The boys thought that was very cool. And after the game, they let fans down on the field as they walk out of the stadium.

Tate and Trey outside "The Trop"

One cool feature at Tropicana is a big aquarium in centerfield where they have real live stingrays on display. The boys thought that was really neat!

A view of the scoreboard and you can see how the turf is looking pretty worn

Trey getting an autograph from Rangers pitcher, Cole Hamels

Pretty good seats and Trey already has his Rays shirt on, but still supporting the Braves

A great shot of the dome above Tropicana Field. Not very aesthetically impressive, but the building was air conditioned!

To enhance the fan experience, they did let fans walk out on the field after the game, which was kind of cool, and the boys did enjoy that.

We were able to get two more stadiums checked off and also take a family cruise in the process. Lots of good times were had and lots of good memories were made. As far as the map goes, we had now covered the entire eastern side of the United States except for one stadium - Nationals Park in Washington D.C.. And we had a different plan for that one which was destined to be an "All-Star Experience!"

CHAPTER 17 - 2017 - SUNTRUST PARK - AND 2018 - FANFEST AND #14 NATIONALS PARK

It had been three years since our last big baseball trip when we traveled around the Great Lakes to take in Cincinnati, Detroit, Toronto, Pittsburgh, and Cleveland. And that brought the total number of stadiums for the boys to 11. Two years ago we went to Florida and saw Miami and Tampa Bay, which were sandwiched around a cruise to the Caribbean. 13 down. In 2017 we decided to take a year off from the big quest to save up some money because the 2018 trip was going to be quite costly.

We did get to experience something pretty special in 2017. We got to see our beloved Braves open up their brand new stadium - SunTrust Park (later to be named Truist Park, which is pretty spectacular in it's own right). We were there for opening day and got to see the Braves get a walk-off win, thanks to Nick Markakis, to beat the Phillies!

We took the year off, if you can call it that, so we could save up for the next big adventure, and that was to get to the midsummer classic, the MLB All-Star Game.

Four years earlier when we started this journey, we were supposed to go to Washington but by the time we were ready to go there, we were so tired we decided to skip that one and come home. My lovely wife (and event planner/coordinator) Tammy, who is always planning for the future, discovered that the All-Star game in 2018 would be played in Washington D.C. She said we could see that stadium when we go to the All-Star game!

Now, I remember thinking at the time that, Yes! That would be so amazing. But then I started thinking that our last name is not Rockefeller or Vanderbilt. There is no way we could afford that. Thus, the year off. And I guess this is where I had underestimated our C.F.O. (Tammy) and her ability to budget properly to make this happen. We had done the research, pinched and saved our pennies and yes, we headed to Washington D.C. for the All-Star Festivities.

We started early, or should I say Tammy got started early on the planning. We booked a week-long stay at a basement apartment in the Capitol Hill section of D.C. on AirBnB. It turns out the place was very adequate even though parts of the neighborhood were pretty sketchy, but I'll elaborate on that later. We purchased our tickets for the 89th MLB All-Star Game on StubHub and the tickets to the Home Run Derby on Vivid Tickets. Now, as I alluded to earlier, we are not the Rockefellers and these tickets were not cheap. And so now college may no longer be an option for Trey and Tate but hey, we are making memories, right? So we packed up the Minivan and headed to the nation's capital.

We arrived in D.C. around 4:00 in the afternoon and I had planned for us to see some of the sights. We decided to see some of the monuments at night since they take on a different look and it would be much cooler. After we find our accommodations and get settled in, we decided to head into town to see the monuments. We walked four blocks down to the nearest METRO station and purchased our cards to ride the subway (yes, it was obvious that we were tourists trying to figure out how to operate the ticketing machines). Now they say D.C. is a walking city, but I had no idea we would have to do SO MUCH WALKING!!

Tate at the Lincoln Memorial

Trey and Tate with the Capitol building in the background

I think that night we walked 4 or 5 miles trying to see as much as we could. We walked from the Capitol down across the mall past the Smithsonian buildings to see the Washington Monument, and caught a glimpse of the White House. Then headed to the World War II Memorial on our way to the Lincoln Memorial past the Korean War Memorial. Then went to the Jefferson Memorial and back to the Subway station. Needless to say, we all slept pretty well that night as visions of the next day's events were dancing in our heads - and that was to go to MLB FanFest at the Washington Convention Center.

We awoke on Sunday morning with anticipation of going to FanFest. After our experience on the subway, which was not too bad the night before, we looked into using Uber. We had never used an Uber before and to be honest, I had some reservations. My brother Joe and his family just got back from NYC and he told me how he had paid $60 for an Uber ride. So, just out of curiosity, I looked into it. I had downloaded the app on my phone and punched in the location we wanted to go to and the location of where we were and voila! We could take an Uber ride to the Convention Center for around $7.00. Wow, that was cheaper than the subway, by far. So with the punch of a few keys on my phone, there was a car waiting outside our apartment in about 5 minutes and it took us to FanFest. I was impressed with Uber and we would use it several more times throughout our journeys.

Now I had no idea really what to expect at FanFest but, was I pleasantly surprised! It was like a Baseball Disneyworld! There were so many cool things to see and do for young and old. And you never knew who you might run into.

The entrance at FanFest

The boys loved the activities at FanFest. There was something for everyone. Trey getting some swings in.

The boys getting an autograph from the late Gaylord Perry

There were Hall of Famers there signing autographs. There were vendors giving away promotional items and then there were the experiences, which the boys really liked. For example, they had pitching machines where fans young and old could participate in hitting, fielding, and throwing activities. There were all kinds of exhibits showcasing baseball history, Negro League history, and Minor Leagues history. There was so much to do that we knew just one day there would not be enough. We decided we needed to squeeze in another day at FanFest. More on that later. As we left FanFest, we were walking to the subway station to get to the ballpark when we were stopped by someone working for Chevrolet and they were running a "Grab a Chevy" promotion. They asked us if we wanted a free ride to anywhere within a 5-mile radius. We told them we were on our way to the Ballpark and they offered us a ride in a new Traverse, which was really nice. And, they gave us each a free 20 oz. Coke since Coke was partnering with Chevrolet on that promotion. Score! Free ride to Nationals Park and a free Coke!

My first impression of Nationals Park was pretty favorable. It was in great shape. It doesn't have the nostalgia that some stadiums have, but it kind of ranks in the middle of the pack of all the MLB stadiums I have been to.

Later in the afternoon at Nationals Park, we decided to attend the MLB Futures Game. Originally we had decided not to go to this event but Tate wanted to go to the Celebrity Softball game, so we looked into it. I used TickPick to find some pretty reasonably priced tickets and we went. It turned out to be a really cool event that was a lot of fun.

Tate at Nationals Park at the Futures Game - Stadium #14

In the Futures Game, many of MLB's top prospects participated in a game of young players from the US vs. young players from around the World. It was a pretty exciting game. We even got to see two of the Atlanta Braves top pitching prospects, Kyle Wright and Touki Toussant. Both played very well and in the game, there was a new record of 8 homers that were hit which doubled the previous record of 4. That is always a good indication of how entertaining the event was for the boys.

After the Futures Game, there was the Celebrity Softball Game featuring people like Jamie Foxx, Disney Star Skai Jackson, Washington Wizards star John Wall, Washington Redskins star

Josh Norman, as well as MLB legends like Tim Raines, Andre Dawson, and Bernie Williams among many others. As an added bonus, we were entertained by D.J. Diesel a.k.a. Shaquille O'Neal. It was an entertaining day and the boys really enjoyed it. So we left the park and again we used Uber. Not bad even though the driver was not very chatty. We got back to our apartment and crashed to get ready for the next day, which was going to be The Home Run Derby!

CHAPTER 18 - ALL-STAR WORKOUT DAY AND HOME RUN DERBY DAY!

After getting back fairly late the night before, we decided to sleep in and lay around a little on Monday morning in preparation for the anticipated late night watching the Home Run Derby. This was a day that we were all looking forward to because, who doesn't like to see a lot of home runs, right? MLB hosts an exhibit called Play Ball Park which provides an opportunity for kids to play wiffle ball at a park right next to the stadium. Tate had participated in it the day before and we were going to let both boys participate prior to going to the ballpark. Monday was a VERY HOT day with temps in the mid-90s so to go and watch the boys play outside in that heat was not something I was looking forward to. Since we had Derby tickets, that also enabled us to get into the Gatorade All-Star Workout Day, which was the event where I thought Trey would have a good chance of getting an autograph if we got there early enough. Well, the workout day started at 5:00 with the gates opening at Nationals Park at 3:00. So, we decided to leave our apartment around 11 AM and go down to the ballpark and have lunch and then go to Play Ball Park and then into the stadium.

So for lunch, we went to a place called Declaration where I had one of the best foot long hotdogs that I have ever eaten. While we were eating lunch, I asked Tammy if she had the tickets to the Home Run Derby. She gave me a strange look and said, "No".

Of course, I thought she was joking and asked, "you're kidding, right?" And then I realized she was not kidding. Panic mode set in! So now we had to scramble around and figure out a way to get back to the apartment and get the tickets and get back to the stadium. All the scenarios were running through my mind about how to do this. Tammy insists that she go get them and that I take the boys to Play Ball Park. So my choice is to figure out a way to get the tickets or go to Play Ball Park with the boys and melt like a snowman in the 95-degree heat. After much deliberation, it is decided that Tammy go get the tickets and I sweat my keister off watching the boys. And wouldn't you know it, Chevrolet saves the day. As Tammy is walking to get on the subway, there is the Chevrolet tent again, offering rides to anyone wanting to go within a five-mile radius. They offer to give her a ride back to the apartment, wait on her, and bring her back to the ballpark! And, they gave her an ice-cold Coke Zero! So, in 25 minutes she has the tickets and is back while I am soaked through with sweat at the Play Ball Park. When she got back, looking all refreshed, I teold the boys it was time to go and we headed toward the stadium.

As we entered the stadium, the boys and I planned our strategy to somehow get an autograph or at least a baseball during batting practice. Our plan was to head toward the right field foul line and get a close look at the All-Stars coming out and maybe get someone to come sign autographs. Unfortunately, no one was signing autographs but we did get to see a lot of the players up close, and we did get a couple of baseballs thanks to some of the pitchers out shagging. Jacob deGrom from the Mets and Ross Stripling from the Dodgers each tossed us a baseball. So, all was not lost I guess.

Trey and I in our Home Run Derby Seats. Trey holding a ball we got in Batting Practice. If you look real close, you can see the Home Run Derby Stamp on the baseball

After the All-Star workout and BP for the Home Run Derby participants, it was time for the Derby. We were able to score two pairs of seats up in the right field section on the second deck. The Nationals promoted these seats as "Home Run Derby Dream Seats" and they did not disappoint. The boys were super excited about the Derby. We, of course, were rooting for Freddie Freeman representing the Braves, but we were actually pulling for any left-handed hitters since we were sitting in the right-field seats. How cool would it be to be on national television catching a Home Run Derby ball? As it turned out, Trey and I sat together and had 3 balls come very close to us, two in front and one behind us, but we were unsuccessful in catching one. Tammy and Tate were in kind of the same situation sitting another section over from us (We decided to split our seats to increase our chances of getting a ball). As luck would have it, as Kyle Schwarber was hitting, one very nice guy caught a ball right behind Tate. So close! But then he gave the ball to Tate!. He was a Nationals season ticket holder and he told Tate he would give him the ball but that he had to become a Nationals fan. Tate then offered to give him the ball back! Way to go, Tate! But the guy relented and Tate was able to take home one of the 114 balls hit in the Home Run Derby. Each Derby ball had a logo imprinted on it to signify that it was a unique baseball.

Tate with the Home Run Derby ball from the guy behind him. Very cool guy! Look at that smile!

It was a great lesson in Human Behavior. Some people were going nuts trying to catch a ball, even to go so far as to knock other people over. So, for the guy to give Tate his ball was really cool. All in all, the Derby was an awesome event and one of the highlights of our trip. It would be hard to top that as far as the level of excitedment that it created. We headed back to the apartment and get ready for the next day's events in anticipation of the 2018 All-Star Game.

Tate, with Tammy, still smiling after the Home Run Derby

CHAPTER 19 - FANFEST AND THE 89TH ALL-STAR GAME!

After the awesome time we had at FanFest on Sunday, we decided that we needed to go back. So I found some more tickets online for about $6 each and we headed back to the Civic Center on Tuesday morning to go to FanFest. We wanted to get there early so we could get a Max Scherzer bobblehead by being one of the first 300 people in the door. (As it turned out, we did get there in time, but the bobblehead was about the size of a small Christmas Tree Ornament) By being there early, the boys were able to participate in a lot more of the activities without having to wait in line. They also were able to get registered to participate in the Wiffle Ball Home Run hitting contest. We were able to get another Hall of Famer's autograph - Rollie Fingers, so that was pretty cool. We also got to meet and have a picture taken with MLB Network's Kevin Millar, who is someone the boys watch every day on the show, "Intentional Talk". As a bonus, we got to witness a Hot Dog Eating contest sponsored by Nathan's Hot Dogs featuring the greatest Professional Eaters on the planet, including the 16 Time Nathan's July 4th National Hot Dog Eating Champion, Joey Chestnutt who set a new record this past Fourth of July when he ate 74 hot dogs and buns in 10 minutes!

The Nathan's Hot Dog Eating Exhibition Contest we got to see up close at FanFest!

The Legend - Defending Hot Dog Eating Champion Joey Chestnut with Trey and Tate

It was quite a sight to see these people devouring so many hot dogs in 5 minutes. According to Tammy, "it was disgusting". But it was quite impressive. For me, it was just so intriguing. And, no surprise, Joey Chestnut was able to defend his crown. The man is an eating machine!

The boys were excited to stop by the Topps Trading cards booth and had their own baseball cards made which they thought was pretty neat. Trey is getting in to collecting baseball cards so this was a very interesting exhibit as they were giving away free promotional cards

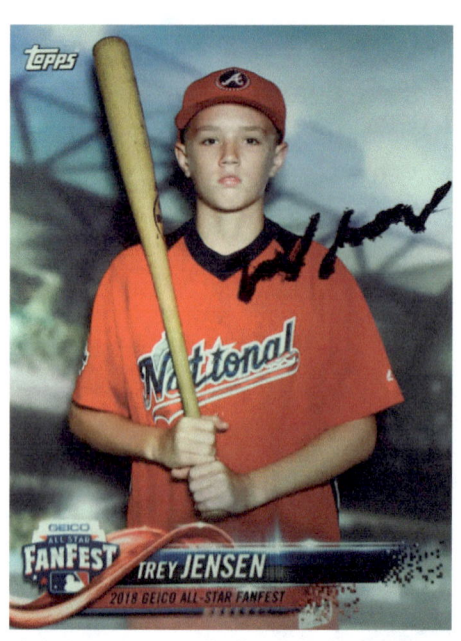

The boys and their Topps Baseball Cards (Trey autographed his!)

The All-Star Game

After our second day at FanFest, it was time to head back to Nationals Park for the 89th MLB All-Star Game. This was, for me, the most exciting part of the trip. The chance for our boys to see so many Superstars at one time was pretty special. We went there early and, as usual, we were planning our strategy to get an autograph or at least a BP ball. Trey and I again went to the National League dugout in hopes of getting an autograph from anyone who would sign, especially any of the Braves players who were there. Unfortunately, no one came out to sign so we decided to go to the outfield to try to catch a ball or get a player to throw us one.

Trey and Tate watching batting practice

After waiting and watching in awe of all of the great players out on the field, we had just about given up on getting anything. It was getting more and more crowded by the minute. To no one's surprise, this was going to be a sold-out event. As the boys were just about fed up and ready to go up to our seats, in stepped Aaron Judge to finish up his BP round. This guy is HUGE. He is a mammoth of a man. He hits right-handed and we were standing in right field so I was not feeling very optimistic, but he is very strong and could hit it out of the park to all fields. Just then, he cracks one toward right field and as I am watching it, I notice that it is coming right towards me. I have my glove on and am popping my fist inside it in anticipation of possibly getting to make a play. As I watch the ball, it is heading right toward me. As it crests and starts its downward path, I notice that it is still carrying and I am ready! I stick up my glove as high as I can because I know there may be some other people who may try to jump in front of me to intercept it. Just then, it lands in my glove and I am squeezing it as hard as I can so no one else knocks it out. I pull my hand back down and...Score! I just caught a baseball hit by Aaron Judge! The boys were standing in front of me and turned around to see that I had the ball in my hand. They were so excited. As I handed it to them and made sure they didn't drop it, I was basking in the glow of being "Super Dad" as I was sure to be their hero now (at least for a little while).

Trey and Tate with the "Aaron Judge Ball"

After batting practice, we go to find our seats in anticipation of watching the "Midsummer Classic", the All-Star Game. We were very excited since four Braves players would be participating with two of them, Freddie Freeman and Nick Markakis being chosen starters for the game.

Our seats in the upper deck on the first base side for the All-Star Game

The game started and we enjoyed all the pregame ceremonies. All the Superstars of the game were represented. It was every young (and old) kid's dream to see all of those big names together on the same field.

Braves Superstar Freddie Freeman

The game was very exciting as far as All-Star games go. There was a record number of home runs hit by both teams with 10 dingers being hit. The game went into extra innings (free baseball) and the American League won 8-6. Even though we were pulling for the National League, we still enjoyed the game very much.

After the game, we headed back to our apartment, taking with us cherished memories of a very special 3 day stretch. The next day would not include much baseball as we would go on some "boring sight-seeing tours" (according to the boys) that Mom and Dad wanted to do. I mean, after all, we were in the Nation's Capital.

CHAPTER 20 - CAPITAL TOUR AND BRAVES/ NATIONALS GAME

The next day after the All-Star Game was spent seeing the sites in Washington D.C. The Social Studies teacher in me was very impressed with all of the opportunities and attractions that we could see. The rest of the family was not as excited, but they suffered through some of the experiences. We toured the Capitol Building and even got passes to visit the White House. We spent some time in the Smithsonian and were able to visit many of the monuments in D.C. The boys were probably a little young to truly appreciate everything but they made the best of it. Besides, we still had another ballgame to see.

Luckily, after the All-Star break, the Braves were scheduled to resume play in Washington to play the Nationals. So we had to take advantage of that. We were very excited to be able to see the Braves on the road. It was just good luck that they would resume their season after the All-Star break in Washington. Tammy made sure that we got good seats right behind the Visitor's dugout so we could see the Braves up close. Of course, we had to be there two hours before game time so we could see batting practice. Again, Trey was hoping to get an autograph or two. We get there as the Braves are starting BP and we hustle on down to get a good spot to try to get an autograph. Unfortunately, that did not work out, but we did get another baseball thanks to Sean Newcombe who threw Tate a ball!

After batting practice, we headed over to our seats which were amazing. They must have been pretty prime seats because three rows in front of us were Freddie Freeman's wife and his young son, Charlie (who waved at Freddie every time he came into the dugout). We were only six rows back which was close enough to get a good view of all the Braves players returning to the dugout.

Ronald Acuna Jr. leading off the game

Tate and Trey at the Braves/Nationals Game

The Braves were able to get a big win against the Nationals which was a great way to end an amazing week. The next day we would head home with fond memories of our experiences in Washington D.C. This trip was incredible! There was so much that we got to see and experience. I know the boys will have some memories that will last a lifetime. It will be hard to top this one.

CHAPTER 21 - 2019 - THE MIDWESTERN TOUR - #15 BUSCH STADIUM

Baseball, a spherical shaped bundle of twine, tightly wound, wrapped in two figure-8 pieces of leather that are bound together by 108 stitches. It is a little over 9 inches in circumference and weighs a little over 5 ounces. It is a rather insignificant object when you think about it. But not at our house. The spring and early summer of 2019 had been dominated by the game of baseball. Trey and Tate both played for their Heritage Middle School team and they had also played travel ball. After those seasons finished up, they have played nearly every weekend since. I just finished coaching the high school team and have been helping out with two travel teams since then. So it is only fitting that when those seasons wind down, we should continue our annual trip to fulfill our quest to see as many major league ballparks as we can before the boys graduate from high school.

For a quick recap, we are currently at 14 stadiums after a two year hiatus where we took one year off and then last year we attended all the MLB All-Star Week activities at Nationals Park in Washington D.C. The 2019 trip would be the most involved yet as far as how tight the schedule would be as well as the number of miles we would be driving. But that has never been a deterrent before. It just makes it more of a challenge. This year, we were going to attempt to see St. Louis, Kansas City, Minnesota, Milwaukee, and both Chicago Stadiums - all in 7 days!!

On Friday, June 21st, we pack up the Honda Odyssey and head out from our North Carolina home at about 8:30 in the morning. We drive just about all day to Fairview Heights, Illinois, which is just about 10 miles from St. Louis where we bed down for the night to see our first game the next day. It took about 12 hours to get there if you factor in all the times we stopped for meals and to stretch our legs. The next day we would be heading to Busch Stadium.

One of the more iconic backdrops is at Busch Stadium with the Arch in the background

The first stop on our 2019 trip would be in St. Louis where we would see at least 3 first ballot Hall of Famers (Albert Pujols, Yadier Molina, and Mike Trout) play. The boys were ready to get started and what a treat we would have. As usual, we headed to the stadium early hoping to take in Batting Practice, but the weather did not cooperate. There were thunderstorms all morning leading up to the 1:15 game, but the weather cleared out right before first pitch which was good for getting the game in but neither team took BP.

Albert Pujols in his first plate appearance since leaving St. Louis.

It did not occur to us as we were planning this trip, but this series would feature the return of Albert Pujols to St. Louis for the first time since he left as a free agent in 2011. So the Cardinal fans really turned out to welcome back their hero who won two MVPs during his time there. It was really cool to see. Every time he came to bat, the fans gave him a standing ovation. And in the 7th inning, Pujols hit a home run and the fans went wild! The amazing part was that the home crowd gave him a curtain call, which is unheard of for an opposing visiting player, but it was really neat to see.

Let me just say how impressed I was by the Cardinal fans. They have one of the most dedicated fan bases of any team in the Major Leagues. I would say that 95% of the people in attendance at Busch Stadium that day had some article of clothing on that was red or said Cardinals on it. It was most impressive. The Cardinals went on to win the game 4-2 and there were 3 home runs hit (Marcel Ozuna, Albert Pujols, and Justin Upton). The kids were allowed to run the bases which Tate participated in (Trey felt like he was too old) and we had a really enjoyable time. Busch Stadium is a very beautiful ballpark. The grandstands are fairly steep, which makes every seat pretty decent to watch a game from. To see the Arch in the backdrop from centerfield is one of the more impressive backdrops in all of baseball. This was stadium number 15 which marks the halfway point to all

30 stadiums. In my opinion, it would rank in the upper third of all stadiums I have been to based on atmosphere, fanbase, and aesthetics. It was a great baseball experience in St. Louis.

Tate on the field preparing to run the bases!

The boys at Busch Stadium waiting out the rain delay

After our time in St. Louis, we got in the car and headed west toward Kansas City.
Historical Side Trip: Before going to Busch SStadium, we (or I) wanted to take a little field trip to the Cahokia Indian Mounds.

This is an archeological site located just east of the city of St. Louis that marked the site of an ancient Native American civilization that existed around the years 1050-1200 AD. This was a civilization that was one of the largest that ever existed in North American history. Not much is known due to the lack of historical writings, but it was a fascinating place for history buffs, not so much for 12 and 10 year-olds.

CHAPTER 22 - #16 - KAUFFMAN STADIUM - KANSAS CITY

On Sunday morning, we awoke to heavy rains in the Kansas City area and we were very concerned about the game being washed out. But fortunately, the skies cleared as we were heading into beautiful Kauffman Stadium. To be honest, I never was a big Kansas City Royals fan and I was not really excited about seeing this game. Especially after just having been to Busch Stadium, I didn't really expect this stop to be that impressive. But I was wrong. Kauffman Stadium is amazing. It has one of the most beautiful backdrops behind the outfield wall that I have ever seen. The waterfalls and open-air views are fantastic. When most people think of baseball in the midwest, the St.Louis Cardinals are always the team that comes to mind, but don't sleep on the Royals. Their fanbase may rival the Cardinals in how they support their team. I thought Kauffman was magnificent!

The spectacular view from our seats at Kauffman!

This game was a special event where they would commemorate the Negro Leagues that played back during the times of segregation. Both teams dressed in the uniforms of Negro League teams that were located close to their respective cities. The Royals wore the uniforms of the Kansas City Monarchs and the Twins wore the uniforms of the St. Paul Gophers. In fact, the promotional give away for this game was Kansas City Monarch hats to the first 10,000 fans.

Tate, Tammy, and Trey in their throwback Kansas City Monarchs caps

Kauffman Stadium has a lot for the fans to see and do. There is a great activity area behind the outfield where kids of all ages can participate in a variety of things like batting cages and clocking their pitches (which Tate said was broken because his speed was not accurate!).

The Human Statue guy was neat (and kind of scary)

While Tate did that, Trey was among the autograph seekers down by the Twins' dugout where he was able to get a few signatures (Jonathan Scoop, Jake Odorizzi, and Luis Arraez). There is a Kansas City Royals Hall of Fame which suprised me as

I was not aware of all the great Royals player in the past. Fans can visit it and it does not require an extra charge. And of course, there is a wide variety of foods and beverages for the fans to enjoy. There was not a sell-out crowd like the one we saw in St. Louis the day before, but the Kansas City Faithful that were there were very supportive of their Royals even though they were not having a very good season. The game turned out to be very enjoyable. The Royals must have been fired up in their Monarchs uniforms as they were able to win the game to upset the first-place Twins by the score of 6-1. We saw two home runs hit - one by the Royals' Hunter Dozier and one by the Twins' Eddie Rosario. After the game, they let the kids run the bases so Trey and Tate took advantage of another opportunity to run on a Major League field.

Tate and Tammy in front of the iconic water fountains in right field

For me, Kauffman Stadium turned out to be most impressive. Maybe because I wasn't expecting a whole lot. But the Royals are just four years removed from winning the World Series and you can tell that the fan base is still pretty charged up. All in all, our time in Missouri turned out to be better than expected. I guess they really did "Show Me" that baseball is pretty special in both St. Louis and Kansas City (See what I did there? Missouri is the "Show Me State"). Another thing that was really nice is that Kansas City has a sports complex where both their baseball and football teams' venues are located right next to each other so they can share parking. And both are not in their downtown areas so the flow of traffic in and out is quite smooth.

Kauffman Stadium on the right next to Arrowhead Stadium - Home of the Chiefs

After the game, we headed north to Iowa where we would stop for the night, but not before going through Kansas City just across the state line into Kansas just to say that we had been to another state.

We crossed over into Kansas for a short time just to say we went to another state

The next day we would head to Dyersville, Iowa to check out the Field of Dreams Movie Site.

CHAPTER #23 - "IS THIS HEAVEN?" - THE FIELD OF DREAMS

On Monday, we headed out of Grinnell, Iowa where we had stopped for the night and made the 2-hour drive toward Dyersville, which is where the Field of Dreams site was located. Yes, the actual movie set that was used to make the movie that debuted over 30 years ago. This was mostly for my benefit as it has always been one of my favorite movies. So, the opportunity of going to see the actual farm and baseball field where the movie was made was too good to pass up. First of all, let me say that you don't just happen by this place. To get there, you have to be going there intentionally because it is located on a remote farm out "in the middle of nowhere". That did not matter to us. We were on a baseball journey and this had to be included. As we were driving to Dyersville and seeing all the vast green farmlands and endless fields of corn, I was reminded of one of the more poignant scenes from the movie.

Field of Dreams in Dyersville, IA - "If you build it, he will come"

It's the scene where Terrence Mann (played by the late James Earl Jones) gave the monologue that would justify Ray Kinsella's (Kevin Costner) crazy idea of not selling his farm to investors after plowing up his cornfield to build a baseball field.

> "People will come, Ray.
> They'll come to Iowa for reasons they can't even fathom. They'll turn up your driveway, not knowing for sure why they're doing it. They'll arrive at your door as innocent as children, longing for the past.
> "Of course, we won't mind if you look around," you'll say. "It's only twenty dollars per person." They'll pass over the money without even thinking about it. For it is money they have and peace they lack.
> And they'll walk out to the bleachers, and sit in shirt-sleeves on a perfect afternoon. They'll find they have reserved seats somewhere along one of the baselines, where they sat when they were children and cheered their heroes. And they'll watch the game, and it'll be as if they'd dipped themselves in magic waters. The memories will be so thick, they'll have to

brush them away from their faces.

The one constant through all the years, Ray, has been baseball.

America has rolled by like an army of steamrollers. It's been erased like a blackboard, rebuilt, and erased again. But baseball has marked the time.

This field, this game -- it's a part of our past, Ray. It reminds us of all that once was good, and it could be again.

Ohhhhhhhh, people will come, Ray. People will most definitely come."

As we drove up the driveway, I have to say there was a sense of nostalgia and longing for the past with images of the movie running through my head. And as we parked and walked out onto the field, it was like we were dipped in magic waters. It was amazing!

Every baseball father's dream - playing with their kids on the Field of Dreams

There is a scene at the end of the movie where Ray gets to meet his late father who comes back as a young player and he finally gets to ask him to have a catch. I always thought how cool that would be if I could have a catch with my boys on that field. Well, we did exactly that and I guess we played on that field for a good half hour. It was a special memory for me and one that I will never forget especially when I see that movie. Hopefully for the boys too.

What a special time that I got to share with my sons!

Trey and Tate on the bleachers by the field

There were no ghostly characters coming out of the corn when we were there, just these two scary guys!

So was it worth the extra 3.5 hours and an additional 160 miles out of the way to go there? Absolutely! As we left there, I remember thinking to myself what a wonderful experience we just had. I don't know if Tammy or the boys felt anything but there was a peace that came over me, almost like I had completed a pilgrimage or something. Athough we only spent about 45 minutes there, I think it will be a stop I will never forget. Then we got back on the road and headed north for Minneapolis, Minnesota.

CHAPTER 24 - THE TWIN CITIES - MINNESOTA #17 TARGET FIELD

After we left the Field of Dreams, we headed north, bound for Minneapolis, Minnesota. When planning for the trip, I reached out to my good friend, Nelson Neale, for advice on where to stay and how best to get around Minneapolis. Nelson and his lovely wife, Rose, invited us to have dinner at his house upon arriving in Minnesota that evening. And I must say, after 4 days of fast food restaurants and hotel breakfasts, it was a welcome treat to have a sit-down meal and good conversation with an old friend who I had not seen in a while. We all had a great time catching up as well as being entertained by their 4-year-old daughter, Grayson.

After a very relaxing evening, we returned to our hotel and were looking forward to some relaxing downtime the next day. We would go see the Twins game the next night. After a leisurely morning of resting and catching up on some laundry, we decided to visit an attraction that Tammy was pretty excited about - The Mall of America.

Whoa! What an impressive place. Every shopper's dream . I don't know how many stores and restaurants there were, but if you can think of any name of a retail store, chances are it was there. And the food choices were too many to count. But to top it all, there were amusement park rides inside the mall. It was incredible and a must-visit place for anyone who comes to Minneapolis.

Yes, that is an amusement park inside the mall!

Tate on an actual log ride!

So after walking around the mall for several hours, we

returned to our hotel to get ready for the game. Once again, our friends, Nelson and Rose really took care of us. They hooked us up with some great tickets for the game that night between the Twins and the Tampa Bay Rays. We headed out to Target Field.

The Ballpark was very nice, as were the people there. It is a great place to see a game. The weather was perfect with temperatures in the mid 70s.

Target Field from where we sat in section 109 - Pretty Nice!

We did arrive early enough for Batting Practice, the first time on this trip, and as you may recall, is very important for the boys. Unfortunately, we did not get any baseballs this time, but a lot of BP home runs were hit.

A Big Thanks to Nelson, Rose, and Grayson for hosting us in Minnesota. We had a great time!

The game looked to be a pretty good matchup between two different teams both at the top of their divisions. The game turned out to be kind of lopsided as the Twins jumped all over the Rays 9-4. The Twins' explosive offense already had double-figure hits by the 4th inning.

The food at the stadium was pretty good. We had fried cheese curds for the first time, which were quite tasty. The boys were excited to see a lot of hits including 3 home runs. Our time at the Twins game was very enjoyable and once again, we thank the Neales for their

generous hospitality and especially to Grayson for the in-game entertainment.

As an added bonus, we were also joined by our friend Ryan Feltis, a pilot with United Airlines, who had just flown in that afternoon and decided to take in the Twins game. He, too, is trying to see all 30 Major League Stadiums and this was number 29 for him (one more to go, Fenway, which he completed in 2024).

We are posing with our friend, Ryan, who was visiting stadium #29 for himself, #17 for us

So, after a "restful" time in Minneapolis, we would head to Milwaukee the next day. 17 Stadiums down, 13 to go. We had a great time in the "Twin Cities".

Target Field was a very nice park and the Minnesotans really like to cheer on their Twins. The fans in the Midwest really have a lot of pride for their teams. I guess that is why it is referred to as America's Pastime. Every region in America comes out to support their teams, but there is a different kind of hometown feel in the Midwest.

Tate and Trey with the standard ballpark pose at Target Field

CHAPTER 25 - WISCONSIN WONDERS, LAMBEAU AND #18 MILLER PARK

On Wednesday morning, we left out early from Minneapolis knowing we had quite a busy day ahead. During the planning of this trip, I had nothing but baseball on my mind. And it was not until I had a phone conversation with my buddy, Brett Huffman (a lifelong Green Bay Packers fan), did I realize that we were going to be very close to the city of Green Bay. Now, as I may have mentioned, Tammy was born in Wisconsin and she and her family LOVE the Green Bay Packers. In fact, I think there is something in the water there that makes every Wisconsinian bleed green and gold. Me, well, not so much, but I do enjoy football history. And Green Bay has a lot of very interesting history. So as I was mapping our trek from Minneapolis to Milwaukee, I looked at how far off the beaten path a drive to Green Bay would take. It turns out it would take a couple hours extra. So we decided to make it work. Trey, who is not a huge football fan, has stayed true to his family roots and does like the Packers. Funny story - we decided to keep this little diversion a secret from him and watch his reaction when we got close and pulled into the parking lot. In fact, since I am a history nerd, we had told the boys that we were taking a side trip on our way to Milwaukee to a famous battlefield (which was technically kind of true, there had been many hard fought battles on the Lambeau gridiron). After all, it wasn't unusual for me to want to see something historical. They bought it. It turns out, we had let Tate in on the secret the night before and he played along very well, but Trey had no idea. Even though the signs on the interstate kept referencing how many miles we had left to Green Bay, Trey was oblivious, which made it that much better when we pulled into the parking lot. He was totally surprised!

Trey was pretty excited when we pulled into the parking lot!

It is a most impressive sight! In fairly small Green Bay, Wisconsin, there is this gigantic, beautiful stadium in the middle of a town that is about one-eight the size of Charlotte, NC. We decided to take the Stadium Tour (naturally). It took about an hour, but it was very informative. It could actually cause someone to change their allegiance to another team to become a Packer fan. I was very impressed, and Tammy and Trey were in awe. So much history, and the pride that everyone there had for their team was incredible.

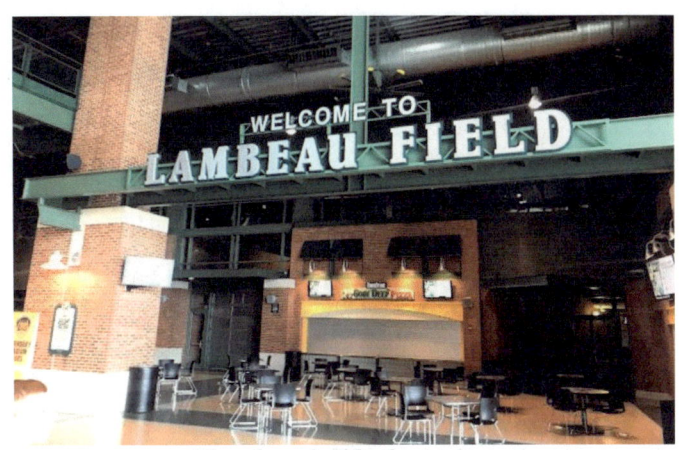

View from inside the Atrium

Our view from inside the Alumni Suite

The view the players have coming out of the tunnel onto the field

The Jensens down near the field at Lambeau! Pretty Awesome!

A very cool stop on our journey!

After an awesome time in Green Bay, we headed south toward Milwaukee and Miller Park, where the Brewers were hosting the Seattle Mariners. This had been a game we had been looking forward to. And we were not disappointed. Something we did notice as we were walking in that we had not seen many other places. Fans at Miller Park tailgate before the games. The were probably Packers fans who look for any reason to hang out and drink beer and roast sausages on a grill.

Miller Park has a retractable roof and for this game, the weather was so nice outside that the roof would be open. It is a beautiful stadium with lots of friendly staff. We get there as soon as the gates open in hopes of possibly getting a BP ball. Unfortunately, we didn't get one during BP because of the layout of the outfield. It was not very good for souvenir seekers to be able to easily get a ball unless the shaggers on the field would throw one to you. So we gave up on that and tried to get autographs. Trey is always on a mission to get as many autographs that he can. He hurried down next to the Brewers dugout hoping someone (hopefully Christian Yelich) would come out and sign. After 30 minutes or so, Tate and I gave up and went to find our seats which were on the Seattle Mariners side of the field. As we get there, a few Mariners players are stretching and just a few autograph seekers are nearby. As soon as we sit down, I see Mallex Smith signing and I tell Tate to go get a ball signed. He walks straight up to him and he signs (and he goes on to have a great game that night too, just a coincidence I'm sure!). Trey was unable to get an autograph and was pretty frustrated, even more so when he saw Tate's signed ball. Trey would rally before we would leave.

Our view at Miller Park (Notice the retractable roof that is open)

Trey, Tate, and myself at Miller park

The game was very entertaining, and unfortunately, the Brewers lost 4-2. We did get to see an unusual occurrence. The Brewers' Ben Gamel hit an inside-the-park home run which is something you rarely get to see. And we got to see Mike Moustakas hit a home run over the right-field fence. The game finished and Trey tried one more time to get an autograph. He spotted one of the Brewers on the other side of the field. He knew immediately by the hair who it was and took off. It was All-Star Closer Josh Hader. I was holding my breath hoping he would still be signing by the time Trey got there. Fortunately, Trey did get a pretty good signature.

Trey with a pretty nice autograph from Josh Hader!

Miller Park was really nice and the people in Milwaukee were so friendly. The stadium was a pleasant surprise and you can really feel the hometown pride of the Brewer fans, not unlike the love that most people in Wisconsin have for the Packers. After a great time at Miller Park, we headed for the exit and got in the car to head south toward Chicago. We were going to Wrigley the next day!

CHAPTER 26 - THE WINDY CITY - #19 WRIGLEY FIELD

Chicago, ChiTown, the Windy City, the 3rd largest city in America. After leaving Miller Park the night before, we decided to make the 2-hour drive down to Evanston, Illinois, just north of Chicago, where we had a two-night reservation. We didn't get checked in and in the bed until after midnight so we slept in a little that next morning. But not too long because we had tickets for a 1:15 game at the iconic Wrigley Field to see the Cubs take on our "red hot" Atlanta Braves.

I was not very excited about trying to get around Chicago due to its large size. We had anticipated using the "El", or the train to make the trip to Wrigley and in fact, our hotel was conveniently located close to a train station. But just for curiosity's sake, I looked into what it might cost to get an Uber or a Lyft. I opened the app and found a ride from the front of our hotel to Waveland Avenue for 10 bucks! Score! We couldn't ride the train that cheap, much less have to deal with getting tickets and dealing with multiple stops. This was a no-brainer. (Shameless plug - The previous paragraph was brought to you by Lyft - the very popular ride-sharing app that allows people to access quick and easy rides to conveniently get around urban areas - For $10 in ride credit, download the Lyft app

using my invite code - YATES48727)

Harry Carey statue on the corner of Waveland Avenue

When looking to buy tickets for the game, we wanted to experience what it was like to be in the famous Bleachers of Wrigley Field, and to sit with the "Bleacher Bums". So when we arrived, we had to stand in line to be able to get seats in the bleachers as they were first come, first serve. We arrive at the ballpark at our customary two hours before the first pitch to get in line before the gates open. We were not first in line by any means. I had really been looking forward to this stop for a long time. I always tell people, when asked which is my favorite stadium that I have been to, that Fenway Park in Boston has been my favorite. And most people will ask, "well, have you been to Wrigley Field?" I would always have to say, "not yet". Well, now I would be able to give my best personal opinion. A little history here, Wrigley is the second oldest stadium in America, being built in 1914 (after Fenway Park built in 1912), and the people on the Northside LOVE their Cubs!

When we get through the gates, you can sense some of the nostalgia of yesteryear as you work your way up to the Bleacher section (kind of like I felt in Boston). And in the areas in the outfield, you do get that old ballpark feeling. The outfield bleachers do have the "old feeling" since it has the old flat benches with no backs for individual seats. We worked our way down to the front row and secured some seats right above the hallowed Ivy of Wrigley Field.

View of the famous ivy from our front row bleacher seats

The iconic manual scoreboard of Wrigley along with our fellow "Bleacher Bums"

I was excited! We were at Wrigley Field and we were going to see our Atlanta Braves. It couldn't get any better than this. And then we started sweating! It was so hot in the bleachers under the blistering sun. But I was soaking it all in. Trey was really enjoying himself getting autographs before the game. This would be his best day ever getting signatures. In fact, he got 9 Braves autographs and had his picture taken with the Braves' Manager Brian Snitker and Braves TV personality Paul Bryd.

Trey with Braves Manager Brian Snitker - "Put me in Coach"

Trey being "interviewed" by Braves TV personality Paul Byrd

The game started out very exciting for us and our fellow Braves fans in the Bleachers as Atlanta went ahead 6-1. But bullpen woes returned and the Cubs came back to go ahead and win the game. There was some excitement just a few feet away from us. When a home run was hit by one of the Cubs, some poor fan in his attempt to catch the ball missed it and got hit in the nose. I think it was broken as there was blood pouring everywhere and he had to be helped out of the stadium by medical staff. We were entertained by Cookie Monster who led the chorus of Take Me Out To the Ballgame during the 7th inning stretch. Another bittersweet moment took place in the 9th inning. Former Brave and All-Star Closer Craig Kimbrel made his Cubs debut that day after recently signing a free agent contract. He came in to try to shut down the Braves and get his first save. It was painful to see him in that Cubs uniform. The Braves, down by two runs, did get two guys on base and then Freddie Freeman grounded out to first to end the game with the score 9-7.

A couple of rowdy Bleacher Bums!

Although the Braves lost, Trey had a pretty good day at Wrigley!

The atmosphere in Chicago was great. Their fans really love their Cubs. We were set to tour Wrigley Field the next day and I would make my final determination about my favorite stadium after that. So even though the Braves lost, we had a really good time at Wrigley. After the game, we went outside the stadium for the picture by the famous marquee at the front of Wrigley Field.

Kind of ironic posing for this with our Braves shirts on

Wrigley was so impressive that the next day we would go back for a guided tour of the ballpark and then head down to a game on the Southside to see the White Sox.

CHAPTER 27 - TOUR OF WRIGLEY AND SEEING THE SOX ON THE SOUTHSIDE #20 GUARANTEED RATE FIELD

After making it back to our hotel from watching the Cubs/Braves game, we decided to order pizza and eat in the room while we enjoyed a relaxing evening just doing nothing. Of course, we ordered some of the famous Chicago Deep Dish Pizza from a local well-known restaurant (for me, it was okay, not blown away by it). The next day we would start out by taking a tour of Wrigley Field and for me, it would be a chance to decide once and for all which is my favorite stadium that I have seen (more on that in a later chapter).

We pack up the van and drive into Chicago on the famous Lake Shore Drive. I am made even more aware of the fact that I am so thankful that I do not live in a city and have to deal with that traffic every day. We arrive early and find some breakfast and then make it over to Wrigley for our tour. It was kind of a rainy and dreary day but the weather improved as we progressed through the tour.

The "Friendly Confines" of Wrigley Field

A lot of upgrades have taken place over the last century

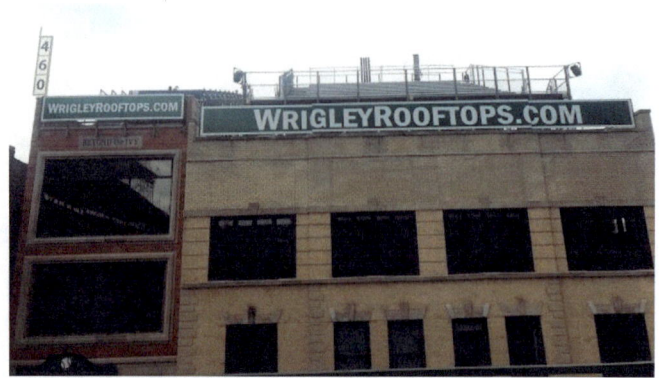

Neighbors trying to take advantage of their priceless real estate selling seats looking over the left field wall (they are not affiliated with Wrigley)

Our Tour Guide's name was Bryan and he was very knowledgeable of the history of Wrigley Field (who many may know was named for the owner of the Wrigley Chewing Gum Company). We learned about the history of the Cubs, whose name has a connection to the Football Team, the Bears. We also learned about the history of the Bleacher Bums as well as the manual scoreboard and the guys that work it every game.

The "Old Timey" manual scoreboard worked by an all male staff

We even got to go up into the visiting team's clubhouse where the Braves had just been the day before.

Tate and Trey sitting where the Braves were just 24 hours earlier!

Then we got to go up to the Press box and see where the Hall of Fame Broadcaster Harry Caray used to entertain the crowd when he sang "Take Me Out to The Ballgame" during the 7th Inning Stretch.

Trey and Tate up in the Booth

We got to go down on the field and into the Cubs dugout which was really exciting.

The boys down on the field (They would not let us on the grass)

Standing in the Cubs dugout

Trey making a call to the bullpen

It was there that our tour came to an end and we headed out of the stadium. The tour was very informative and full of lots of history which I really enjoyed. There was some construction going on at the time which kind of took away from the nostalgia of the old ballpark, but I have to say Wrigley is a must to take in for any baseball enthusiast. Unfortunately, after taking in all of Wrigley, it still does not overtake Fenway as my favorite of all the stadiums so far.

We stopped by Wrigleyville Dogs to have a hot dog for lunch. Then we left the North Side and headed down toward the South Side of Chicago to get ready for the White Sox game that night.

To be honest, after visiting Wrigley, I was not expecting to be very impressed with seeing the White Sox. Everyone always talks about the Cubs in Chicago and there is not a lot of talk about the Sox until you get to the South Side. I'll have to say, though, I was surprisingly impressed with Guaranteed Rate Stadium, even though the name is terrible. Why couldn't they somehow keep the Comiskey name attached to it somehow like they did at Wrigley? But the people on the South Side really do like their White Sox. There is something to be said about the crosstown rivalries that exist in Major League Baseball. But of all the stadiums that we went to on this trip, I would have to say that Guaranteed Rate was probably the most fan-friendly, especially when it came to food. Their selections were by far the best to choose from and the prices were also more affordable. The White Sox were not doing very well this year but you would not know it by watching the game that we saw as we once again saw the Minnesota Twins (for the third time this trip).

The view of the home plate area at Guaranteed Rate Field

The stadium was more open and not as cramped as Wrigley, maybe since it was much newer. There was a kids' area with lots of activities to keep them entertained. Tate took advantage of those as he was able to get in a little practice.

Tate getting in some swings at the Kids' Zone

A view of the Chicago skyline from the "South Side" at Guaranteed Rate Field

Since the White Sox were not having a very good season, we were able to score some pretty good seats right down next to the field for a pretty decent price.

The view from our front row seats - not too bad!

The scoreboard at Guaranteed Rate Field with a rainbow overhead

After a little rain shower blew through, it turned into a very nice, comfortable evening for baseball.

A beautiful night for baseball as the White Sox hosted the Twins

Stadium #20 for Tate and Trey

Since this was the last stop on our 6 stadium tour of the Midwest, we decided to leave a little early to beat the traffic and head for home to get out of Chicago. The game was very entertaining and the White Sox were able to get the win. This had been an amazing trip but like all good things, our trip was about to come to an end. We left Chicago and drove for about two hours where we stopped in Lafayette, Indiana to rest for the night. The next day we would be going home.

We are now 2/3 of the way from completing our quest. And from here on out, it would not be so simple as just jumping in the family van and heading out on a new adventure. To complete the Ballpark Tour from here on out, we would have to fly somewhere and rent a car which will require a little more planning (and money). But we are bound and determined to do this. We've got four more years to get 10 stadiums out west. To be continued...

CHAPTER 28 - 2021 - COVID BREAK AND #21 COORS FIELD - COLORADO

Recap: We began this bucket list adventure way back in 2014 when we were inspired to attempt this goal of visiting all 30 MLB ballparks by the time that our oldest son, Trey, graduates from high school. In 7 years, we have seen so many stadiums. In 2014, Trey was 9 and Tate was 7, we went to Philadelphia, New York Yankees, Cooperstown for the HOF induction ceremony when Greg Maddux, Tom Glavine, and Bobby Cox were inducted, Boston, New York Mets, and Baltimore. In 2015 we went to Cincinnati, Detroit, Toronto, Cleveland, and Pittsburgh. In 2016, we went to Miami, cruised the Caribbean, and went to Tampa. In 2017, we took a year off to save up for All-Star Week. In 2018, we did the All-Star game in Washington D.C. In 2019, we went to St. Louis, Kansas City, Minnesota, Lambeau Field, Milwaukee, Chicago Cubs, and Chicago White Sox bringing the total of stadiums visited to 20 out of the 30, 2/3 of them covered. And then COVID-19 hit in 2020 and everything was put on hold. So, in 2021, as the boys were now 16 and 14, we decided to resume our quest and head out west for Stadiums #21 - #23, Coors Field in Denver, Globe Life Field in Texas (Arlington), and Minute Maid Park in

Houston.

This trip will be different because we would not have our own transportation. It had now become impractical to try to drive to these cities out west. And since the stadiums on this trip are so far apart, we will have to fly into one city and fly home from another. so we flew to Denver, Colorado and get there on Wednesday, June 30. Now, as these trips get farther and farther from home, there is a lot more planning that goes into preparing for them. As I have said before, Tammy is a logistical genius when it comes to planning, so prior to the trip, we thought we have everything covered. Well...when we got to the airport, we had to take a shuttle to the rental car location where we had reserved a car from Thrifty. As we tried to get our keys, we were told that since this was a one-way rental (pick up in Denver and drop off in Houston), we had to put a $500 deposit down on a credit card. We had already paid for the rental car ahead of time. They just needed a credit card to put a deposit on hold. Here is where we encountered a huge difficulty. We did not have a credit card. We had debit cards which work as credit cards on most purchases, but no credit card. The rental agency would not accept a debit card. So, we were stuck. We had to take the shuttle back to the airport and get an Uber to take us to our hotel. (Fortunately, Tammy had a contact with Enterprise who came to our rescue, but it took two days to get it). So we relied on Uber and Lyft and Lime Scooters for transportation to Coors Field and to get around Denver for two days.

The boys enjoyed our alternative modes of transportation, especially the scooters!

Day 2 in Denver - due to lack of transportation, we did not get to do some of the things we wanted to do on this day, but we did go into the city and saw some of the sites. We did discover something unexpected. We happened upon the National BallPark Museum which is a museum dedicated to some of the old historic ballparks that are no longer in existence (Ebbets Field, Shibe Park, Old Yankee Stadium, Polo Grounds, etc.). While on a Stadium Tour, we had to go see this museum, right? I thought it was very good and I highly recommend anyone visiting the Denver area to check it out. They had lots of exhibits and artifacts from many of the torn down parks, so many that The Hall of Fame in Cooperstown has called it one of the best collections of baseball memorabilia. It was a great way to spend some time before the game and it was not too far of a walk from Coors Field. Another thing we discovered in Denver were electric scooters! The boys, especially Tate, were amazed that you could just come upon a scooter, hop on and go (of course there was a small fee incurred after a credit card swipe, but many cities are using these as a way to help reduce emissions - Lime, Uber, and Lyft are all in on this).

The Game - Rockies vs. Cardinals - back when we got our tickets a couple of months ago, I was kind of surprised at how expensive the tickets were going on Stubhub and other sites. Also on the Rockies website, there were not a lot of tickets available. I was wondering why this game was in such high demand, after all the Rockies are not playing that well and they were playing the Cardinals. It turned out that the game we had decided to attend was going to be the first time that former Rockies All-Star Nolan Arenado would be back at Denver. This is not the first time that we were able to experience this as we were able to be in St. Louis two years ago when Albert Pujols came back there for the first time when he was with the Angels. And just like in St. Louis, the Rockies fans gave Arenado a standing ovation prior to his first at bat. He is still held in high regard by Rockies fans.

Coors Field - Wow! We were very impressed with this stadium. I don't know if it is the clean mountain air or maybe the effects of a possible contact "Rocky Mountain high", but this park was beautiful. I purchased some tickets on the third level and as you can see in the pics below, we had an awesome view.

The view from the third level was amazing!

View of the Field from our seats. This was taken after the game had been delayed by rain, but once the skies cleared, the views were gorgeous!

Evergreen trees native to Colorado made up the batter's eye in centerfield

The boys sporting their Rockies T Shirts they got at the Team Store

The game was delayed about 45 minutes due to a passing thunderstorm, but once the skies cleared, the game was underway and you could not have asked for a better night for baseball. The temperature at first pitch was 64 degrees! Some of the highlights of the game:

-It was really cool to see the Rockies fans give Nolan Arenado a standing ovation. They still love him in Denver!

-We saw future Hall of Famer Yadier Molina play for the Cardinals as well as one of my favorite pitchers - Adam Wainwright.

-We got to see home runs hit by Brendan Rodgers for the Rockies and Paul Goldschmidt for the Cardinals.

The Rockies won the game in the bottom of the 9th on a home run from Catcher Elias Diaz (but we were not there to see it as we left in the 8th inning to get back to our hotel making sure that we could get an Uber - yes, Trey was not very happy about missing that!)

All in all, Coors Field did not disappoint. I don't know if it is one of our Top 5 stadiums that we have seen, but definitely is in the Top 10. Maybe I will give my own rankings when we complete this. Denver is a great city. The people are friendly, the air is clean, and the views of the Rocky Mountains are incredible. So we leave Denver the next day and "head for the mountains" for some sightseeing.

CHAPTER 29 - HEAD FOR THE ROCKIES!

On Friday, we left Denver and headed west to go take in some of the sights in the Rocky Mountains. We did not have a whole lot of time to see some of the best places so I decided to go to Red Rocks and then make the hour-long drive to Mount Evans and drive on the highest paved road in North America knowing we could enjoy some beautiful scenery on the way. We were not disappointed. Red Rocks and the famous Red Rocks Amphitheater were impressive. The huge Red Rock formations were beautiful to see and almost made us feel like we were on another planet.

The view of the Denver skyline from Red Rocks

Trey and Tate at the appropriately named Red Rocks

The Red Rocks Amphitheater where famous acts have performed since the 1930s

Mount Evans is one of the Rockies' "14ers" which rises to 14,000 feet above sea level, so we got to see some marvelous views.

It is about 14 miles of continuous winding roads to get to the peak of Mount Evans. It even rises above the tree line and the views as well as the fact that there are no guard rails on the sides of the road are breathtaking!

A view from the road - No Guardrails!

Trey and Tate at the summit

Being with Tammy makes me feel like I'm on top of the world!

One of the things that I have come to realize is that while completing this quest, we have been exposed to so many unbelievable adventures along the way. Our country is blessed with so many beautiful places and one can really start to appreciate it on this trip. So, after our time in the Mountains, we needed to head South toward Texas. We drove a few hours admiring the Rocky Mountains that could be seen from the interstate and got a room in Pueblo, Colorado for the night. Little did we know what not-so-fun times we were going to have the next day!

CHAPTER 30 - AMARILLO BY (EVENING) SORRY, GEORGE STRAIT

After spending the night at the Econo Lodge in Pueblo (NOT RECOMMENDED!), we got up and went to Cracker Barrel for breakfast. We had planned to drive to Amarillo, Texas to stay for a couple nights in the Texas Panhandle. Tammy had wanted to go for a walk along the Pueblo riverwalk but the boys did not seem too interested, so we decided to drive on to Texas for what we thought was going to be a 5-hour drive (it's a good thing we did leave early). The drive south through Colorado was beautiful with the Rocky Mountains always on the horizon to the west. We even got a pretty good look at Pikes Peak along the way. Then we crossed into eastern New Mexico for a while and we headed through the Raton Pass toward Texas (I remembered Clint Black singing about the Raton Pass in his song, The Goodnight-Loving, about a famous cattle trail). As we were coming down and almost out of the Raton Pass, there was a lot of road construction. We were just about to reach the exit where we were to change roads when we hit a huge pothole. Wham! And we punctured a tire.

This was not good!

Our little Mazda 3 that we were driving had these low-profile tires which do not give much when you hit a pothole on the interstate. So we took the next exit which was only .7 miles away and we pulled off into a service station. We called Enterprise to inform them of our dilemma but they were going to be no help as the closest place they could help us was 90 miles away. It was near lunchtime on Saturday of the 4th of July weekend. Most of the nearby Tire Dealers were closed. And those that were open, many did not have the 18" tire that we were needing. We were stressing! So, the boys and I put on the spare (which was a life lesson for them as I had never done that with them before).

We were thinking we were going to have to drive several hundred miles on that spare when we had one more idea. There was a nearby tire store called Cunnico Tire there in Raton. We had called them before but no answer. So, we decided to just drive by there just to see if anyone was there. As luck would have it, it was a little three-man shop and they were open for another 20 minutes. I asked if they had the size tire that we needed and they did not have the exact tire, but one that would work! Thank goodness!

The boys and I outside the tire store that helped us out

So we gladly purchased a tire (which Enterprise reimbursed us for) and went to a nearby pizza place for lunch. Crisis averted. We then headed on t Texas bound for Amarillo. And yes, I made "Tate the DJ" play George Strait's classic song, "Amarillo by Morning" along the way.

We had booked an AirBnB in Amarillo and we got there around 5:00. Tammy had to get a walk in, so we found a local park and she walked and the boys got some long-toss throwing in at the same time. After a long and stressful day, we rested well that night.

CHAPTER 31 - A COUPLE OF DAYS IN AMARILLO

The stadiums on this trip were not very close to each other at all and we knew there would be a lot of driving. So to break up the trip, we decided to find a place to stop to spend a couple of days to rest and recharge while we tried to find some interesting things to do. We had booked an AirBnB for two nights to stay in Amarillo, TX which we found out was the halfway point on the famous Route 66 Highway that runs from Chicago to Los Angeles. It was a famous route for Dust Bowlers in the 30s when they were trying to get to "California or Bust" as well as the road made more recently famous for kids in the Pixar movie "Cars". The boys were familiar with that as they were big fans of the movie, so there was some relevance for them. I just had to see some of the "Mother Road". Unfortunately, there is not a lot of it left since Interstate 40 came along in the late 50s and 60s (which was kind of the back story in the Cars movie). There were some old streets that are in town that are trying to hang on to the past and you can still see the iconic road signs.

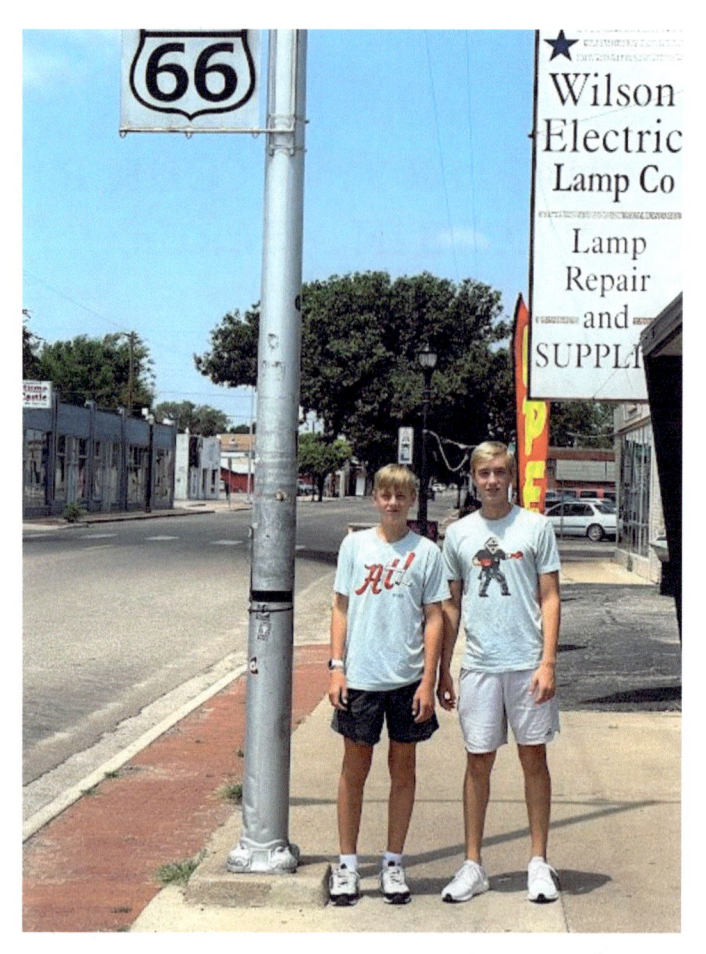

Tate and Trey standing below the iconic Route 66 road sign

Our first stop on our day visit in Amarillo was the Cadillac Ranch. Some guy thought it would be a good idea to bury several old Cadillacs in the ground in his corn field and let travelers come by and spray paint them. It was pretty popular as many people were there even after heavy rains had made it very muddy.

The Cadillac Ranch - notice the cars buried nose down in the dirt

Tate leaving his mark

Trey was here!

So, after we visit that tourist attraction, we head into town to see what was left of Route 66. There is one stretch in town that has become an antique and restaurant row through Amarillo. Sad, but not much there to see. We had a little time so we went to check out the Amarillo Zoo. It had been a while since the boys had been to a zoo, so we decided to check it out. There were quite a few cool animals there (Lions, Tigers, Bears, oh my! And buffalo and elk). After our outing, we went back to the room and prepared for my big treat - Dinner at the famous Big Texan Steak Ranch!

All the way to Amarillo, there were road signs advertising the World Famous "Big Texan". Legend has it that this restaurant owner was feeding some hungry cowboys one day and there was a challenge to see who could eat the most one-pound steaks that he sold. One cowboy ate 4 and a half steaks, a loaded baked potato, a salad, and a dinner roll all in under an hour. This gave the owner an idea. If anyone could come in and eat that same meal, they could eat for free. And, so that is the big attraction there. Over 10,000 people (just over 10%) have done it since the

1960s - eaten a 72 oz. steak with all the sides!

The "Big Texas" - the picture does not do it justice

The boys outside The Big Texan

You've got to love a restaurant with the phrase steak ranch in their name!

My meal - only a 16 oz. ribeye - Pretty darn good!

After our meal, we decided to, what else, go see another baseball game! Amarillo is the home of the Amarillo Sod Poodles, the Double-A minor league team for the Arizona Diamondbacks. This was also the 4th of July and they were hosting a fireworks show after the game. The game was nearly sold out and all we could get were standing-room-only tickets. The ballpark was amazing. The team and the stadium were only two years old so everything was really nice. What is a Sod Poodle you may say? Well, it is a nickname for a prairie dog. The game didn't go so well for the home team as the Wichita City Wind Surge blew in and was able to pull out the win. It didn't matter. A good time was had by all and the fireworks were great!

The Amarillo skyline from the ballpark and yes, Jason Aldean, it was an Amarillo Sky - absolutely beautiful!

After the game, we headed back to our place and prepared for the next day's 5-hour drive to Arlington to see the Texas Rangers.

CHAPTER 32 - ARLINGTON, TEXAS - #22 GLOBE LIFE FIELD - TEXAS RANGERS

On Monday morning we left Amarillo and drove southeast to Arlington. We leave the Texas Panhandle to make the 5-hour drive. You really get an idea of how big Texas is when you start driving across the state. We arrive mid-afternoon and find our hotel which is within walking distance to Globe Life Field. (Stadium Tour Tip - pay a little more to stay within walking distance to a stadium if you can - it is much more convenient and the parking is already taken care of) Globe Life Field, MLB's newest ballpark (at the time of this writing) had been built and opened in 2020, so I was excited to see what it was like. The number one feature that it has - air conditioning! It is an indoor facility and to watch baseball in the AC is pretty nice, especially in the Texas heat!.

Another good thing about staying within walking distance for Tammy was that she did not have to go to the game the same time that we did. We always like to go in as soon as you can, which is usually two hours before first pitch to watch batting practice. Tammy got to stay behind and do her workout and come to the game a little later. We were about a half-mile from the stadium which was about a 10 minute walk.

The view of Globe Life Field as we were walking in. It is located right beside Globe Life Park which is the old stadium - it looked to be in great shape, but no AC!

Inside Globe Life Field - very impressive and the inside temp was amazing!

The Rangers were hosting the Detroit Tigers, which was not exactly a marquee matchup as both teams were near the bottom in their respective divisions. The game did have some interesting storylines:

-Kolby Allard was the starting pitcher for Texas. He was a former Braves prospect that was dealt to Texas the previous year. He pitched a great game into the 6th when he gave up 5 runs. But until the 6th, he looked sharp, striking out nine.

-Former Hickory Crawdad, Joey Gallo, hit a home run in this game. He would also be in this year's Home Run Derby the next week in Colorado. Other home runs hit were by Texas catcher Jonah Heim and Tigers shortstop Zach Short.

The Tigers went on to win the game 7-3. The game was enjoyable, mainly because the temperature inside was perfect. The prices at the stadium were some of the highest we had seesn. Concessions and merchandise prices were on the high end compared to many places that we have been (they do say everything is bigger in Texas, including prices apparently).

The "Boomstick" hot dog - we didn't try it but looking back on it, we probably should have

I was able to get front row outfield seats, but we had to look through these wires

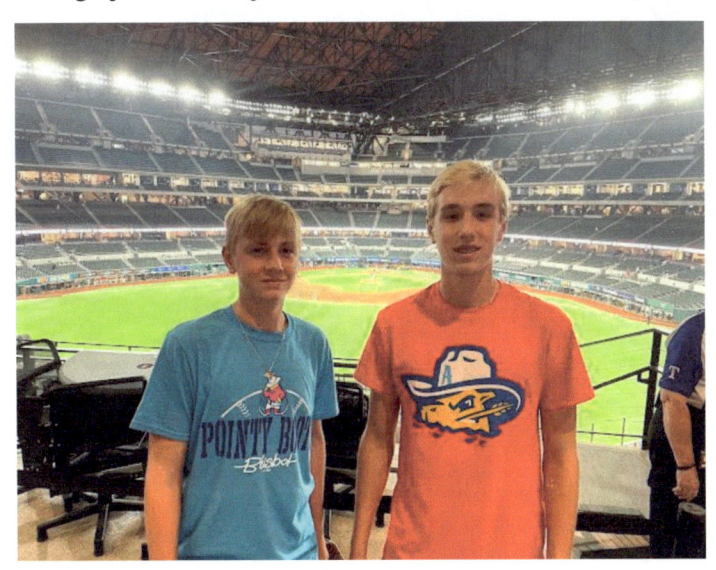

The boys sporting their Sod Poodle shirts at the Rangers game

All-in-all, the Rangers game was fun. The facilities were great and the atmosphere was very pleasant. I don't know that it really stands out to me as a must-see ballpark due to the fact that it is an indoor facility, but in the Texas heat, air-conditioning is a must-have, which kind of takes away from the traditional ballpark feel for me. Stadium number 22 checked off the list. The next day we were off to Houston.

CHAPTER 33 - STADIUM #23 - HOUSTON ASTROS' MINUTE MAID PARK

On Tuesday, we left Arlington and made the 3-hour drive to Houston. We were able to reserve a room at the Cambria Hotel which was a fairly new hotel in downtown Houston and only three-tenths of a mile to Minute Maid Park. The hotel was very nice and we scored a city-view room on the 18th floor - very nice! We checked in around 3 and rested a while before going to the game. The tickets for the game I had acquired through FaceBook on the Astros Ticket Exchange group page. This is highly recommended (thanks to the tip from my brother-in-law Chantz, whose family had lived in Houston). By purchasing through this group page and using Paypal and the Ballpark App, there are no hidden fees like you might pay through Stubhub. Anyway, I got two sets of seats - one pair in the famous Crawford Boxes in left field and the other pair was on the front row in right field. The night before we left for Houston I received a message from one of the season ticket owners that I bought the tickets from. She told me that for this homestand against the A's that the stadium was opening up 30 minutes earlier for season ticket holders! Perfect - now the boys and I could get in to watch most of the Astros batting practice as well as the A's - what this means is a better chance of getting a

BP ball or two (we ended up getting 4!). And Tammy could stay behind and go to the fitness room and still have time to shower and get ready for the game.

Small World - before the game as Tammy was coming into the par, she met a family from Taylorsville, NC (about 45 minutes from our home) - The Pierce Family - who are also on their bucket list mission to see all the MLB ballparks. They were really nice folks who were at Minute Maid (#13 for them) and then they were heading on to Arlington and then to Omaha for a baseball tournament that thier kids were playing in. We were able to share some stories about different adventures that our families have had on this journey. It was great to meet people who have shared similar experiences.

So again, we were able to see a game in an indoor facility that had air-conditioning. This could spoil you because it was really nice (especially compared to watching some games in "Hotlanta"}. The game featured the AL West Division-leading Astros vs. the second-place team - the Oakland A's.

The view from our seats in the Crawford Boxes

My attempt at taking a "selfie" with Tammy

The game was very exciting, but one highlight of the night for me was the fact that it was a Tuesday game and that meant "Dollar Dog Night!" A promotion the Astros have is that on Tuesdays, all Nolan Ryan Hot Dogs are $1 and you can get as many as you want. This was awesome! We all ate our fill!

The A's jumped out to an early lead, but the Astros came from behind to win 9-6 thanks to 2 home runs by the Astros' rising star - Yordan Alvarez. Halfway through the game, Tate and I decided to switch seats (I think so he could get away from Trey who can be quite bossy to his little brother). Funny tidbit - As fate would have it, Yordan's second home run was hit into the Crawford Boxes right in the direction of where Tate and Tammy were sitting. Now, Tate had his glove with him and might have had a chance to catch the ball, but he did not have his glove on when the ball was hit. Needless to say, he did not catch the ball even though it might have been within reach. He was in an aisle seat and it landed in the aisle. Of course, his brother has given him grief ever since. We even watched the highlight of Tate NOT catching the ball on MLB Network several times.

Astros Mascot Orbit waving the victory flag

Standard Stadium pose for the boys with the field in the background

So the Astros won the game and we headed back to our hotel to prepare to fly back to Charlotte the next day. Stadium number

23 in the books! This adventure, although somewhat stressful at times, was a memorable one. We got to see some of the beautiful scenery that our country has to offer as well as see some pretty cool ballparks. I'm not exactly sure yet about where these three parks would rank as far as favorite parks go. I guess it depends upon the criteria. I plan on writing about that later. The next trip(s) will be much more involved as we will have to fly and drive again out to the west coast. But this trip was full of some pretty incredible memories - ones that we will look back on for years to come.

CHAPTER 34 - 2022 - THE WEST COAST - THE GRAND CANYON

It was the Summer of 2022 and we were now in the ninth year of this adventure of trying to see all 30 Major League Ballparks by the time Trey graduates from high school. Trey just finished up his Junior year and we are now heading into the home stretch. Up to this point, we have seen 23 stadiums and each year gets more and more challenging. Last year we went to Denver and to Arlington and Houston. This year we are starting out in Phoenix and then heading west into California to San Diego, Anaheim, Los Angeles, San Francisco, and Oakland - leaving just Seattle for next year right after Trey's graduation. If you look back through the pictures, you will notice that the boys have changed quite a bit since 2014. Both are now almost grown and we started this when Trey was 9 and Tate was 7. As usual, there will be some side trips that we will take on this trip. And props again to Tammy for planning this trip. It will be quite involved and by now, she is a real Pro!

On Wednesday, June 22nd, we flew out of Charlotte to Phoenix where we picked up a rental car and headed North toward one of the greatest side trips, maybe, of this whole adventure, The Grand Canyon. Fortunately, we had no problems this year with getting a one-way rental. I don't care what anybody says,

Phoenix is a very hot city. I think it was 104 degrees when we landed (and again I don't care - it may be a dry heat, but it is still amazingly HOT).

We had decided ahead of time that since we are going to be in Arizona that we should make the drive North and see the Grand Canyon. It was a 3 and a half hour drive up to Grand Canyon National Park, which was a very interesting place. I'm sure seeing the Grand Canyon is on most people's bucket lists and it certainly was on mine. The boys did not seem too interested in seeing it - besides we are out here to see baseball games. But I think once we go there, they were pretty impressed!

On Wednesday, our first day in the Park, we went immediately out to see the Canyon. It did not disappoint! It is magnificent. I don't think the pictures really do it justice.

Tammy, Tate, and Trey taking in the sights

On Thursday, we decided to make a day of visiting the park and we wanted to do a hike down into the Canyon. The boys were in good shape and Tammy works out and I had been walking some so we thought we would start out with the 1.5 mile Blue Angel Trail. Now, 1.5 miles does not sound like a lot, but when you are descending 1000 feet during that 1.5 mile hike, it can be quite a challenge. And as you would imagine going down was not too bad. But coming up was VERY DIFFICULT. It took about 40 minutes to go down and about an hour to come back up. Needless to say, we were drained!

The boys as we prepare to head down into the canyon

Tammy at the beginning of the descent

The views were breathtaking (or it might have been the hike!)

We encountered a Mule Train caring supplies up the trail

It was not uncommon to see Elk in the park - even in the town of Tusayan, AZ where we saw this very tame 7X7 Bull Elk eating grass along the sidewalk

Needless to say, the visit to Grand Canyon National Park was definitely worth the extra effort, and one that I highly recommend. After our hike, we headed back to the hotel and cleaned up and got some dinner and decided to go back to the Grand Canyon for an event called the Grand Canyon Star Party. We were able to see a pitch black sky with more stars than I had ever seen. There were over 50 astronomers there that had set up telescopes focused on various stars and constellations. We got to see some pretty cool views of stars and also got some lessons in astronomy. I thought it was interesting. The rest of my family was not as impressed. So we headed back to the room and bedded down to head back to Phoenix the next day. My take on the Grand Canyon - another place in our great nation that is very difficult to describe with words other than to say, it was awesome!

Next up - back to Phoenix for the Diamondbacks game.

CHAPTER 35 - PHOENIX AND #24 CHASE FIELD - ARIZONA DIAMONDBACKS

After leaving the Grand Canyon, we made the 3.5 hour drive south back to Phoenix where we would go see the Diamondbacks that night. We made pretty good time getting into the city and had some time to spend before we could check into our hotel. The temperature in Phoenix when we arrived was again was about 104 so there was nothing much that we could do outside so we decided to go see a movie. The boys went to see the new Jurassic World movie and Tammy and I went to see Elvis! It was outstanding! I give it two thumbs up. Austin Butler nailed the role. He will win the Best Actor Academy Award. Write it down! (As it turned out, he did not win in 202, but was nominted)

After the movie, we checked into the hotel and set out on the half mile walk to Chase Field. Maybe not the best idea as the temperature was pushing 106 on the walk (some would say, "but it's a dry heat", I don't care - 106 is still 106). We got in and basked in the AC at Chase Field!

Chase Field - Home of the Arizona Diamondbacks - Stadium #24

The Diamondbacks were taking on the Detroit Tigers so the number of people in attendance was kind of small but the fans that showed up were very supportive of their DBacks! And there were a few devoted Tiger fans in attendance as well, many sporting Miguel Cabrera jerseys. It was kind of cool getting to see the future Hall of Famer (Cabrera) play and get a hit. The highlight of the game was watching Tiger infielder Javy Baez hit a Grand Slam!

The Tigers went on to win the game although the Dbacks put up a pretty good fight. Our seats were in the outfield as we had 2 seats in left field and 2 in right. Below are some of the views that we had.

Chase Field - View from Home Run Porch in centerfield

Tate and Trey at Chase Field - sorry about the lighting - Tate sporting his Serpientes (Diamondbacks Spanish Heritage) T-Shirt

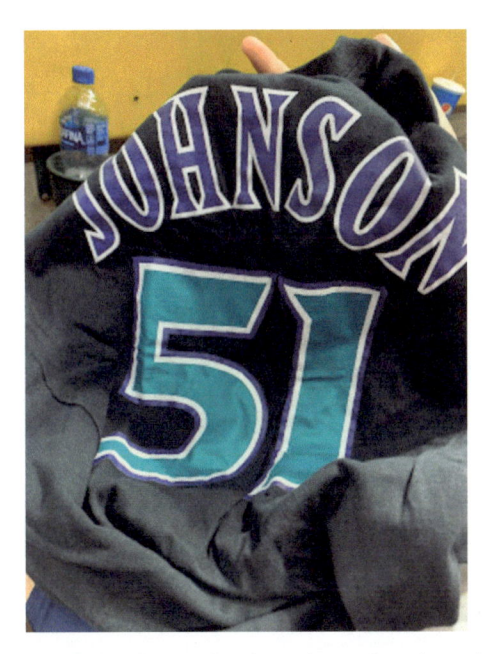

Trey's T-shirt he got in Phoenix - "The Big Unit"

Chase Field is a nice ballpark. It is like an Oasis in the middle of a desert - literally! The amenities were very nice. I don't think they could play unless it was indoors because the heat would be unbearable. The people were friendly and they were very supportive of their team. It's difficult for them in that they play in one of the most challenging divisions in all of Major League Baseball having to battle the Dodgers, Giants, Padres, and Rockies. But it is a nice place to watch a game.

We headed back to the room again walking a 1/2 mile at 9:30 and it was still 97 degrees! Unbelievable! The next day we would head to San Diego!

CHAPTER 36 - SAN DIEGO AND STADIUM #25 - PETCO PARK

Sunny San Diego and #25 - Petco Park was one of the stadiums that we were really excited to see. It has hosted the All-Star Festivities in the last few years and has a reputation for being a really nice ballpark. We were set to see a Sunday afternoon game against the Philadelphia Phillies. When we scheduled the trip, this game was one that we were excited about because of the major talent that would be on the field. The Padres have one of the most exciting players in the Majors in Fernando Tatis, Jr and another young star in Manny Machado. The Phillies have the reigning National League MVP - Bryce Harper. Unfortunately, neither of those guys played because they were injured. That didn't matter, the ballpark was going to be exciting. We stayed in a hotel at Coronado Beach which was located across the San Diego Bay from downtown San Diego and Petco park. We got up early, had breakfast, and got on the Ferry to ride across the Bay to the San Diego Convention center and made the short walk to the Park.

*Trey and Tate on the ferry crossing the bay with the
San Diego skyline in the background*

Petco Park (street view)

The view from where Tammy and I sat. We were in full shade - which was nice - except for Tammy who got cold!

The Western Supply Building on the left

The mezzanine behind the stands - notice the Southwestern style which was prevalent throughout.

The game was very entertaining. We got to see Yu Darvish pitch for the Padres. In the end, it was the Phillies who pulled out the victory, but we enjoyed the game and thought the ballpark was amazing. It may be in my personal Top 5. We will have to see when we complete the task.

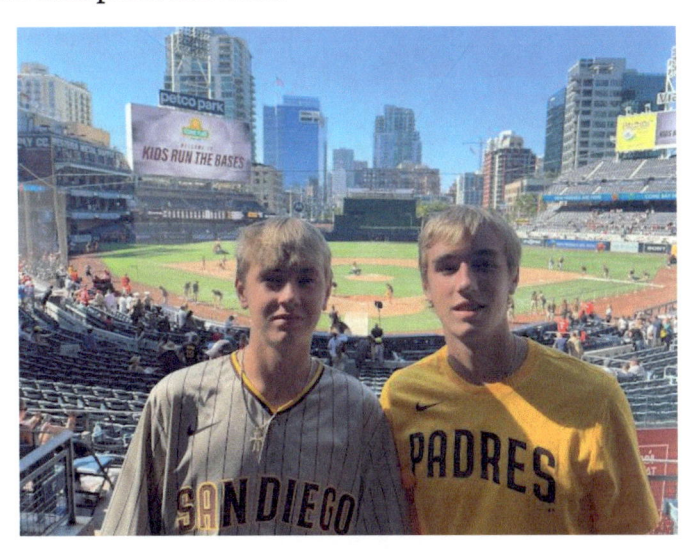

Tate and Trey wearing their newly purchased Fernando Tatis Jr. Jerseys

San Diego was really nice. The Park was beautiful with lots

of things for the fans to do. There is even a grassy berm beyond centerfield for those that wanted to sit on the grass. Unfortunately for us Braves fans we did not want to see the Phillies win, but we had a great time. San Diego is a nice town and to sum it up, I will quote Alejandro, our Lyft driver who took us back to the hotel. "It is pretty chill" to live in San Diego. I couldn't agree more. For those of you that know me and my humor, I'll wrap up this chapter with another quote, this time from Anchorman Ron Burgundy, "You Stay Classy, San Diego!"

We went back to the hotel and watched the Braves take on the Dodgers on TV. That game did not end well either. The next day we would head north on the PCH to Anaheim for a game at Angels Stadium.

CHAPTER 37 - THE PACIFIC COAST HIGHWAY AND #26 - ANGELS STADIUM

On Monday, we were set to drive up to Anaheim to see the Angels. Before we left Coronado/San Diego, we found a park where the boys were able to get some throwing in as both are still in the middle of their showcase seasons.

The boys getting a little "long-toss" in at a park in Coronado to keep their arms in shape

I was not looking forward to the drive into the outskirts of Los Angeles by taking I-5 all the way in. So we decided to take a more scenic route via the famous Pacific Coast Highway, Highway 1, as it is referred to. It was more scenic but the weather did not cooperate. It was very hazy, or maybe smoggy that day. We would continue on that road as we left LA heading to the San Francisco Bay area later in the trip. Hopefully the weather will be better. We did spend some time at Huntington Beach, which was nice but as the pictures indicate, it was very overcast and hazy there too.

After some time at the beach, we headed into Anaheim and check in to our hotel to rest up before we go to Angels Stadium. This was a game the boys were looking forward to because they were going to see two of the best players in the Majors - Mike Trout and Shohei Ohtani.

Angels Stadium was surprisingly a very nice ballpark. It was a little dated, but some of the features there in the design, especially the outfield, make it very appealing.

The entrance to Angels Stadium features two caps, size 679 ½!

The entrance at Home Plate Gate was pretty impressive

The boys had to get a Shohei Ohtani Jersey - and yes, we have been asked if they are twins (which Trey does not appreciate!)

The rock formation with waterfall was quite an impressive feature beyond centerfield

The boys were excited to see the GOAT - Mike Trout - but on this night, he went 0 for 5 with 3 K's (Even the best can have a bad night I guess)

The Angels were playing the Chicago White Sox with Noah Syndegaard (LAA) taking on Lucas Giolito (CWS). The game went back and forth. No home runs were hit although there was an exciting play in right field that appeared to be a homer but was challenged and determined to be a triple. The Angels went ahead in the 7th and held on to win the game. As seen in the pic below, the rock feature is also highlighted when the Angels win!

Fireworks and flames to punctuate the victory!

To me, Angels Stadium was most impressive. It is somewhat dated and they are desperately hanging on to their last World Series victory, which was in 2002. This season they were celebrating the 20th anniversary of that accomplishment. I would think it is very hard to compete with their next door neighbors just 30 miles up the road (The Dodgers), but the fans that were there are devoted and the employees are very friendly and helpful. We had an issue with our tickets and Patti at Guest Relations went out of her way to accommodate us. I was pleasantly surprised with this park and would probably have to put it in my Top 10. We headed back to our room which was a mile walk. The next day we would be driving up into LA to see the sights and take in Hollywood!

CHAPTER 38 - "I LOVE LA!" - TOUR OF THE SITES IN LOS ANGELES

On Tuesday, we slept in a little and took our time to head out of Anaheim and headed up I-5 into Los Angeles. We were going to spend three nights in LA and we had booked an AirBnB to spend a little downtime and recharge our batteries. The AirBnB was phenomenal and just what we needed after a week on the road. We made a quick grocery run to Target and actually got to cook some home cooked meals for a couple of days. Since there is so much to see in Los Angeles and we did not have a lot of time nor any local knowledge, we decided to book an all-day tour to see as much as we could. Tammy booked us a tour with www.adayinlatours.com and we had to drive into Hollywood to be picked up at 8:00 AM. We got up early, made breakfast and were parked at the Dolby Theater parking deck at the designated time. The tour turned out to be very good and our guide was excellent. Colin was very knowledgeable and entertaining and we got to see a lot of the well known sites! Here are some of the highlights:

The tour started at the Santa Monica Pier and Venice Beach.

Tate felt right at home at Muscle Beach!

The Chez-Jay Restaurant, a half block from the beach which has been in operation since 1959 where just about every big name in Hollywood has eaten. Legend has it that the Rat Pack hang out here on Thursday nights to play poker and that Marilyn Monroe and JFK would meet here.

Venice Beach, which at one time had over 60 miles of canals just like Venice, Italy. Now it has about three miles of canals left, but it is very "artsy" and is a popular place for skateboarders.

Venice Beach is a very eclectic kind of place - graffiti on palm trees is okay!?!

Next we went into Beverly Hills and got to walk up and down Rodeo Drive (pronounced RO-DAY-OH for all you that may be unrefined and unfamiliar)

Yes she is!

The Via Rodeo, a cobblestone street that runs up from Rodeo where more high-end shops can be seen

We went to the Hollywood Farmers Market at the Grove for Lunch.

Then we made the drive up to the Griffith Observatory where we took in the beautiful views of the Los Angeles Skyline and got the best look at the famous Hollywood sign.

Our best view of the famous sign that was originally "Hollywoodland"

Our view of Downtown LA from the Observatory

Our tour concluded with the Hollywood Walk of Fame and Grauman's Chinese Theater where the stars put their hands in cement. Colin pointed out all the cool places along the way and we were very pleased with what we were able to see in such a short amount of time.

One of my favorite actors honored in 2006

To qualify for a star on the walk of fame, someone has to stay "relevant" for 5 years in movies, tv, music, production, or stage

For anyone that does not know much about the Los Angeles area, I would highly recommend splurging for a tour to see the most iconic places during your stay. After a whirlwind tour of Los Angeles, we headed back to our stay to get some rest for the next day when we would go to Dodger Stadium.

CHAPTER 39 - #27 - DODGER STADIUM

This one had me feeling all types of emotions as we were preparing to visit. First of all, as a Braves fan, I don't particularly care for the Los Angeles Dodgers. I wouldn't go so far as to say that I hate them (although there have been times when that word might have been accurate, especially when it comes to their unlimited budget and ability to sign almost any free agent that they want). But in my lifetime as a Braves fan, there have been periods of time when the Dodgers were our nemesis. And then there is the whole Freddie Freeman free agency debacle. So I tried to have an open mind prior to the visit. And then there is the traffic situation. Everything I had read online said do not drive to Dodger Stadium, but our place that we stayed was only 4 miles from the ballpark. It was just a good idea to leave early (which is no problem for us). We left 2.5 hours before first pitch and it's a good thing we did. Traffic was not terrible, but just to be safe we got inside pretty quickly which gave us more time to explore the ballpark.

Dodger Stadium is the third oldest ballpark in the US (behind only Fenway Park in Boston and Wrigley Field in Chicago). It opened in 1962 and this year, 2022, they were celebrating their 60th anniversary. It is a giant of a stadium and seats 56,000 people. The game featured the Dodgers taking on their division rival the San Diego Padres, which led to the game being sold out

- over 53,000 people were there! I think 52,000 were Dodger fans. I was very impressed with the show of support from the people there that LOVE their Dodgers. I don't think I have seen anything like it in that large of a scale. I could not help but think that it is no wonder that the Dodgers have so much money to sign free agents. Dodger Stadium is a money making machine! And 90% of the fans had a Dodger Jersey and hat on!

The awesome view from Dodger Stadium!

The stadium was magnificent! The weather was great with temperatures in the low 70s at first pitch and actually got down into the mid 60s before the game was over. It was Trea Turner bobblehead night and we picked up 4 of those (Tammy and Tate had sold theirs in the first 5 minutes - Tammy got $20 and Tate got scammed for $10). The game was entertaining and the Dodgers won 3-1 thanks mostly to Justin Turner's two home runs. As I referred to earlier, it was pretty tough seeing Freddie Freeman down there playing first base for the Dodgers. And then we had to see another former

Brave Craig Kimbrel come in and get the save.

The views of the mountains in the background of Chavez Ravine especially when the sun goes down are amazing. The food options were quite impressive but I decided to go for the famous Dodger Dog and Garlic Fries which were pretty good. Trey and Tate had the bucket of Chicken Fingers and pound of fries.

The famous Dodger Dog - my thoughts on it...meh!

Yes, we did wear Braves attire at Dodger Stadium, except for Tate who had his Padres Jersey on, that's how we roll!

Former Brave, Freddie Freeman - Yes, it was too soon!

Tate and Trey at Dodger Stadium - Tate broke down and got a Clayton Kershaw jersey (who else for a lefty pitcher?) and Trey was still repping the Braves!

The traffic situation leaving the ballpark took a little while, but when you have to get 53,000 fans out of there, it is bound to take a little time. We were back at our place after the game in about an hour. All in all, Dodger Stadium left quite a good impression. For me, it has definitely launched itself into the Top 5 Stadiums. 27 down and two more to go on this trip. The next day we left LA and headed up the coast for San Francisco.

CHAPTER 40 - SAN FRANCISCO AND #28 - ORACLE PARK

On Friday, July 1st, we left LA to make the 6 hour drive north to San Francisco. We had hoped to take the Pacific Coast Highway but we were under a time constraint and had to be checked in and at Pier 33 in San Francisco for the Alcatraz Tour. This was a little side trip that Tammy was looking forward to and at one point we did not know if we would make it. So, I put the hammer down and we made it into San Fran with 45 minutes to spare. The temperature in LA and throughout most of the drive was in the mid to upper 90s. When we get into the Bay area, the temps begin to drop quickly. When we arrived at our hotel near the Fisherman's Wharf, the temperature was in the 60s. It is a different climate in Northern California in the Bay area for sure.

So we get checked in and put on sweatshirts and sweatpants! We get to the pier and get on the boat for the Alcatraz tour. "The Rock" as it was known was a federal prison for nearly 30 years and housed such notorious criminals as Al Capone, George "Machine Gun" Kelly, and Robert Stroud, "The BirdMan of Alcatraz", to name a few. The tour was very informative, although most of the tour was about the Native American takeover of Alcatraz from 1969-1971, but by that time the prison was shut down. It is/was a very remote, dreary, and desolate location. It was kind of neat to get to see what some people had to experience. After the Alcatraz tour, we went down to Pier 39 and ate supper at a Bubba Gump's restaurant (which was where Tate wanted to go). Then we headed back to our room to get ready for a 1:00 game the next day.

On Saturday, we got up, had a great breakfast at the Hotel Riu, and began making our way to Oracle Park, Home of the San Francisco Giants as they were set to take on the Chicago White Sox (who we saw play the Angels a few days before). I was excited to see this stadium as I had heard a lot of good things about it. So we dressed warmly in our sweatshirts and sweatpants and headed for the ballpark.

Our view walking into Oracle Park

It was a very cool day for July (probably in the upper 60s and overcast), but we were somewhat prepared. As we entered the stadium, we realized it was Lamont Wade Jr. bobblehead day so we each got one of those upon entry. Since we were not big Giants fans (and we did not have room in the luggage to tote them back) Trey sold his inside for $5, Tate traded his for an old A's Matt Chapman bobblehead, and Tammy traded hers for a Buster Posey coffee mug. We kept one. We walked around the ballpark to see the sights. Oracle Park is a magnificent stadium. The design is very unique as you can hopefully see from the pictures.

The view from where Tammy and I sat

Tate and Trey near their front row seats down the left field line

Trey and Tate overlooking the famous McCovey Cove just beyond the right field wall

Levi's Landing in right field

The view of the scoreboard and outfield area with so many interesting features

We splurged a little on the seats, splitting up our group into pairs again. The boys got to sit right on the front row down the third base line and had a great view of the Giants players, especially former Brave Joc Pederson who played LF for San Fran. Tammy and I sat in the Lower Bowl section down the first base line, but I would think that there was not a bad seat in the park.

The game went by very quickly as Giants starter Logan Webb carried a no-hitter into the 5th and then things began to unravel. White Sox starter Dylan Cease gave up a leadoff home run to Lamont Wade (on his bobblehead day!) and then settled in. The Sox went on to win the game but we really enjoyed Oracle Park. All of the stadiums in this trip up to this point have been very nice. San Francisco is a great baseball city and we really enjoyed our time there. The next day, we would see some sights around the Bay Area and prepare for our last stop on the trip, in Oakland.

CHAPTER 41 - #29 - THE OAKLAND COLISEUM

On Sunday, we decided to take some time and drive around the area surrounding San Francisco to see some of the most popular sites. Our first destination was to go to the Golden Gate Bridge. We had to drive through the streets of San Francisco to be able to cross the bridge. We got to see some of the famous hillside streets that San Fran is known for and made our way across the bridge to the Golden Gate Park to take some pics and then had to come back across to make our way down the Pacific Coastline that we were anxious to see.

After seeing the Golden Gate bridge, we headed back south toward Highway 1 down through Pacifica, Half-Moon Bay and into Santa Cruz. Wow! What a beautiful drive! We got to see some of the most beautiful coastline that I have ever seen. Hopefully, the pics will do it justice.

Tate and Trey in front of the Golden Gate Bridge

Picturesque views of the PCH - Pacific Coast Highway

After we went to Santa Cruz, we decided to go see some of the famous California Redwoods. We drove to a state park just outside of Santa Cruz to see the trees. They are quite impressive. Unfortunately, we did not see the Giant Redwoods, but the ones we did see were pretty cool.

After we got back, we looked forward to a little downtime at the hotel. The next day we would be going to see our last stadium on this trip (Oakland Coliseum) and then we would be heading home.

On July 4th, we made our last stadium trip to Oakland Coliseum where we would watch the Oakland A's take on the Toronto Blue Jays. We were not very excited for this stadium except for the fact that this was the last one. The Oakland area was a little more sketchy compared to the other cities that we had been in. But we went there with an open mind. The A's had not been having a very good season and attendance had not been good either. But this was July 4th and they decided to put on a promotion to get fans in the seats. They decided to offer second level seats for $7.04 each (July 4th, 7/4) which included an opportunity to go out on the field after the game and watch a fireworks show! Well, since we had splurged a little at some of the earlier parks, second level seats were just fine with us.

Our view of the stadium while walking in.

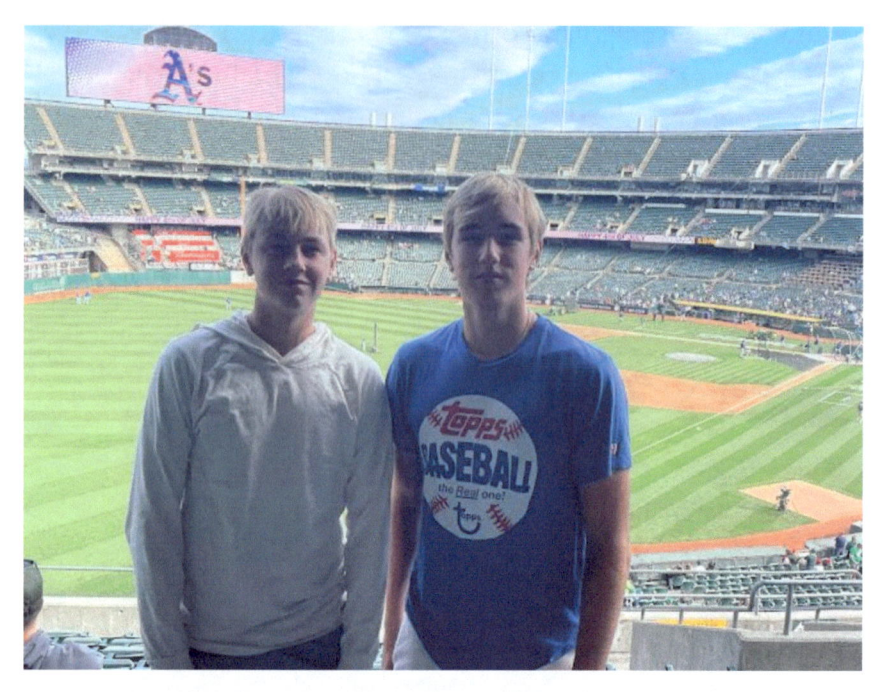

Tate and Trey with the standard stadium picture pose from our seats

Not a bad view for $7.04 (July 4th Promo) each!

The Oakland Coliseum is one of the oldest parks in the MLB and we were not expecting a whole lot, but I have to say, I was pleasantly surprised! Even though it was old and very big (it supposedly seats more people than any other stadium at over

56,000) I thought it was a pretty neat place. Of course it was very dated and kind of stuck in the 1970s, but I thought there was a good view of the field from just about anywhere. I know this because in about the 5th inning we moved up to the third level (to get away from the crowd which finally started coming in to get ready for the fireworks). Oakland fans, even though there were not many, like all other fans are very passionate about their team, which I could appreciate. The attendance was probably around 30,000 due to the fireworks show coming up after the game (they had been averaging around 5,000).

The game was exciting as the A's played very well and went on to win, maybe because the extra fans had them motivated. And after the game, we headed down to get ready to go out onto the field to watch fireworks. I have to say, anytime I can get out on to a Major League field, I get pretty excited. I get that Ray Kinsela feeling wondering "is this heaven?", but very quickly I realized that, "no, we were still in Oakland!

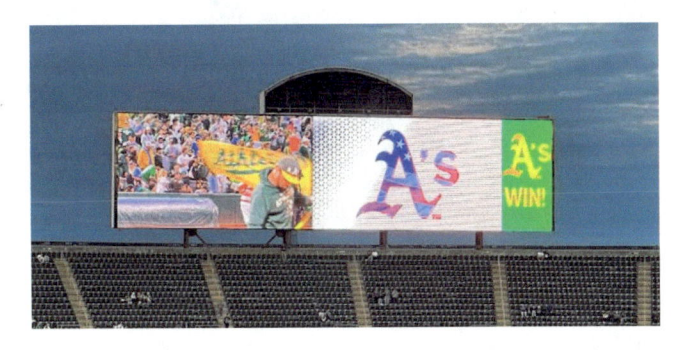

We got to see the A's get a win which did not happen much that season

The Field is named for Rickey Henderson, the Hall of Famer who played in Oakland for many years.

The fans poured onto the field after the game for a great view of the 4th of July fireworks

The fireworks show was very good! It was set to patriotic music and the crowd was into it and I thought, what a great way to end our trip. After the show, we headed out to find our car and then we made the 25 minute drive to the airport for the trip home.

We had an early morning flight out of San Francisco the next day so we decided to spend the night in the airport which seemed like a good idea at the time. Looking back on it, I would not advise that as there are not many comfortable locations to try to get a little sleep inside an airport.

But that did not spoil the trip by any means. The West Coast trip was a great adventure. We had gotten to see so many iconic places and, as a whole, it might have been one of the best stadium trips we've been on. So as far as MLB stadiums go, 29 down. 1 to go - Seattle. That would be the plan for the next year. We may have to do something to make that trip extra special. Top it off with an Alaska Cruise maybe? To be continued...

CHAPTER 42 - 2024 - THE EMERALD CITY #30 - SEATTLE'S T-MOBILE PARK

What started 11 years ago with what at times seemed like an impossible dream sparked by a Hall of Fame induction came to fruition in the Summer of 2024 with the completion of a bucket list adventure for our family to see a game at all 30 Major League Ballparks. It was a huge challenge and took longer than originally planned. We started this in 2014 and the goal was to complete it by the time our oldest son, Trey, graduated from high school. Well, he graduated in 2023 and due to many difficult family losses that year, we had to postpone the completion of our quest to another year. We had one park left - Seattle. And as you know, for someone living in North Carolina, getting to the Pacific Northwest posed a real challenge. But we planned and saved and budgeted and decided to get it done in August of 2024.

But this trip was not just going to be a trip to see a ball game. We decided to finish this quest of making memories by finishing it up in style. After seeing a game at T-Mobile Park in Seattle, we would then get on a Norwegian Cruise ship and go on a 7-day Alaskan cruise! This was going to be an epic trip. On Wednesday, August 8th, with the threat of Tropical Storm Debby coming in from the Gulf of Mexico and drenching the Deep

South, we flew out of Charlotte on a 5 1/2 hour flight to Seattle.

On the approach into Seattle, we had a great view of Mt. Rainier!

Upon arriving at the airport, I got my first experience with a company called Turo. Rather than deal with a rental car company, you can now rent people's cars from them directly, just like you would rent a house on AirBnB. Tammy had used this service before when she had gone on a trip to Wisconsin and she was very happy with how the process worked. So we tried it again. We picked up our car that was left at the airport parking garage and off we went to find the AirBnB that we had booked for our 3 night stay in Seattle.

We arrived at our place and found it to be quite accommodating and comfortable. We then headed out to get some dinner at a local Chinese restaurant and picked up some groceries at an Amazon Fresh, which was a pretty neat little grocery store. We headed back to get some rest as the next day we would go downtown to see the sights and check out the city, and check off number 30!

Of course in Seattle there are a few attractions that you must see. The first stop was the Pike's Place Market. It was packed with so many vendors peddling fresh vegetables, crafts, baked goods, and of course, seafood. The market took up probably 3 blocks down along the waterfront next to Puget Sound. It was bustling with activity. We picked up a few things and grabbed some lunch trying out some of the local seafood.

Pike' Place Market

The busiest place of all was probably the shop billed as the original Starbucks, which some of the locals will dispute saying that the original shop was a little farther away, but it did not deter the dozens of people waiting in line out the door to get in.

The original Starbucks?

Next we made our way a little farther north to find the Space Needle, the iconic attraction built for the 1962 World's Fair that many people think of when they think about Seattle. At one time the 605 foot high tower was considered the tallest structure west of the Mississippi. It was an impressive sight and a huge attraction as so many people were there. The surrounding areas are like a carnival in that many shops and vendors try to lure in the many patrons of the Space Needle. As you may recall from our St. Louis trip, I am not a big fan of heights and I was not about to go up in that thing. But Tammy and the boys were excited to go up. So they bought their tickets (at $40 a pop!) and got in line while I found a Starbucks and got me a coffee and found a shady spot to sit down and listen to the sweet sounds of a Guatemalan Pan Flute Band (They were great, Zamfir would have been proud).

The World Famous Space Needle - 605 feet tall!

The boys "hanging out" 600 feet up!

After a busy morning and early afternoon, we were feeling a little "Sleepless In Seattle", so we decided to head back to our place and get a little rest before heading to the ballpark.

On Thursday, August 8th, we entered ballpark #30 on this great quest that we had started on back in 2014. To accomplish it in 2024 was a year behind schedule, but all in all, it was such a good feeling to be able to say, "We did it!" The game featured the Seattle Mariners taking on the Detroit Tigers in what would turn out to be a very entertaining ballgame.

Tate and Trey outside waiting to enter ballpark #30 - T-Mobile Park!

T-Mobile Park was a pretty cool place to see a game. They do have a roof that will open and close depending on the weather. On the day we were there, the Seattle weather was wonderful, about 75 degrees and no rain so the roof would be open. We made our way in and this game was one of their "value games" so tickets were fairly affordable. We got seats behind home plate for about $45 each which was a great deal.

View from our seats - Incredible!

The game was a pitchers' duel at first and we cruised through the first 6 innings very quickly. The Tigers managed to pull ahead 3-1 heading into the bottom of the ninth. It was "rally time" as we kind of wanted our monumental game to be a little more exciting. And the Mariners delivered! The M's were able to get the bases loaded and then Mitch Haniger came to the plate with 2 outs down 3-1 and he hit a double to right center field scoring all 3 runners enabling Seattle to walk it off by the score of 4-3. How fitting for the game at our last ballpark to end in a walk-off!

Mariners Walk It Off!!!

Stadium #30 of 30! - WE DID IT!!

As the game ended and we were walking out, there was such a tremendous feeling of accomplishment that I felt as I was trying to wrap my mind around what we had just accomplished as a family. It was almost inconceivable at the time when we set out to do this in 2014. I have to give my wife Tammy all the credit on this one. She is the one who threw down the challenge. I was just excited about going to a Hall of Fame induction. She took it to a whole different level. And what a collection of memories and stories that we have to tell. In that 11 year time span, baseball has become a major part of our family. Both boys have played all through middle school and high school as well as during the summers in travel ball and showcase ball. They have had amazing careers so far as Trey and Tate both have been selected as the Player of the Year in their high school conference. Trey is now playing in college at Lenoir-Rhyne University and Tate will be finishing up his high school career next season.

Many people may not understand why we did this, but when your kids have a passion for something, sometimes, as parents, we tend to go overboard. And maybe we did, but what an amazing adventure it turned out to be!

After the game, we went back to our AirBnB for the night. The next day we would go back for another game since we had a couple more days in Seattle. We got seats in the outfield and I have to say, that game was not as stressful for some reason. After all, we had checked the box so all that was left to do was to just sit back and enjoy the game which we did because the Mariners beat the Mets, always a pleasure for any Braves Fan!

A couple days later, we did get on a boat and took that Alaskan cruise. It, too, was an amazing adventure and a great way to top off our vacation. But as I look back, I am so proud of all that we accomplished on this quest. We got to see so many interesting places and meet so many wonderful people along the way. The boys, who were both very young when we started this, really do not remember much about the early years and they want to start over. I'm not so sure about doing this again, but there are some places that I would like to see again as well, someday. But for now, we have some great memories as a family that we will always carry with us. Although it was a tremendous challenge, to anyone that is a baseball fan, I would highly recommend doing this with your family. It was incredible!

CHAPTER 43: "THE WALK OFF"

The most exciting ending of a baseball game is a walk off victory. It involves someone from the home team getting a game-winning hit to score the deciding run to win the game. Not that I think that I'm going to end this story with an exciting jaw-dropping revelation or anything, but I am going to try to answer the question that we were always asked when we told others about our quest, "which ballpark has been your favorite"? So now that we have completed the mission, we now can have a valid opinion after having seen them all. It is a fair question, but somewhat of a loaded question. Because we are usually asked by someone who has their own opinion or allegiance to a certain team or city. We, too, have allegiances and it is not such an easy question to answer. It really all comes down to personal opinion. So, to answer the question, I'm going to give my personal opinion.

In considering which ballpark or stadium is my favorite, I've kind of categorized my response. I tend to have a reverence for the older, iconic parks. Probably not a big surprise coming from someone who studied and taught American History for over 30 years. To me, there is just something nostalgic about the older ballparks, especially the ones that have such rich histories and stories that so many people are familiar with. Fenway Park in Boston, Wrigley Field in Chicago, and Dodger Stadium in Los Angeles are definitely fixtures in my Top 5 list. Each of those are so impressive and each has gone to great lengths to preserve their rich histories and yet make it appealing to contemporary tastes.

The next category that I use is how aesthetically appealing a ballpark is. There are many ballparks that have such interesting features and marvelous views that it's almost like being in a dream when you walk in. Places like Oracle Park in San Francisco with its really cool outfield view of Levi's Landing and the huge "old-timey" mitt in left-centerfield. Or Coors Field in Colorado with its breathtaking views of the Rocky Mountains in the distance and the evergreen trees beyond centerfield and the purple color scheme that pairs well with the plush green outfield grass. And then there is Petco Park in San Diego that incorporates many southwestern styles in their decor and color schemes that goes well with the mostly sunny weather that seems to be a constant in San Diego. At Pittsburgh's PNC Park, views of Roberto Clemente Bridge dominate the landscape beyond the outfield wall and their use of black and gold unifies all the major sports teams in the "Steel City". At Angel Stadium in Los Angeles, I was very impressed with the Rock Waterfall beyond centerfield. All are very nice places to watch a ballgame. Then there are the stadiums that I call the "throwback parks". These are the modern stadiums that try to bring back some of the more appealing components of the older ballparks. They tried to make them blend in to their surroundings and incorporate neighboring properties rather than demolish them. Camden Yards in Baltimore is a good example as is the previously mentioned Petco Park in San Diego, The Great American Ballpark in Cincinnati, CitiField in New York, and Minute Maid Park in Houston.

I am not crazy about the roofed or convertible stadiums although most of them are necessary due to the climate where they are located. Even though the temperature is very comfortable, and there are no rainouts, to me, they are just kind of "meh" compared to all other ballparks.

I am going to try to come up with a Top 10 List. So, here goes:

My Top 10 List

Yates Jensen's Unofficial Top 10 MLB Ballparks (and maybe some that should be):

    1. Fenway Park - Boston

2. Wrigley Field - Chicago
3. Dodger Stadium - Los Angeles
4. Camden Yards - Baltimore
5. Coors Field - Denver
6. Oracle Park - San Francisco
7. Petco Park - San Diego
8. PNC Park - Pittsburgh
9. Minute Maid Park - Houston
10. Truist Park - Atlanta

HONORABLE MENTION
Yankee Stadium - New York
Busch Stadium - St. Louis
Guaranteed Rate Field - Chicago
Angel Stadium - Los Angeles
Great American Ballpark - Cincinnati
Miller Park - Milwaukee
Safeco Field - Seattle

I know many might disagree with my list and if you asked me on a different day, more likely, my list might be different. But at the end of the day, it doesn't really matter. Everywhere we went, the fans were incredible. The hometown crowds were loyal, dedicated, and supportive of their teams. And that was probably the biggest takeaway. No matter where we went, there was such a strong feeling of devotion to their teams. And most of them had a great respect for the game. Baseball really is the "Great American Game". If you have stayed with me this far, I want to say "Thank You". It is an honor and I hope you enjoyed our story. So, I encourage you to get out there and go to a ballgame. Maybe I'll see you at the ballpark sometime!

The End

ABOUT THE AUTHOR

Yates Jensen

Yates Jensen is a retired high school history teacher and baseball coach as well as a life-long Atlanta Braves Fan. He and his family have a passion for the game of baseball. In 2014 they decided to try to see a game at all 30 Major League Ballparks before their oldest son graduated from high school. They completed their quest in 2024. This is their story

Made in the USA
Columbia, SC
25 January 2025